100
THINGS TO DO IN
ITHACA
BEFORE YOU
DIE

Cayuga Waterfront Trail

100 THINGS TO DO IN ITHACA BEFORE YOU DIE

AMANDA JAROS CHAMPION

REEDY PRESS

Reedy Press
PO Box 5131
St. Louis, MO 63139, USA
reedypress.com

Library of Congress Control Number: 2024939062

ISBN: 9781681065380

Design by Jill Halpin

Printed in the United States of America
24 25 26 27 28 5 4 3 2 1

DEDICATION

For Rob,
the best thing I discovered in Ithaca

Indian Creek Farm tomatoes

CONTENTS

Music and Entertainment

Sports and Recreation

Culture and History

Shopping and Fashion

ACKNOWLEDGMENTS

Thank you to Reedy Press for giving me the opportunity to create this book. It has been a joy to look at Ithaca again with new eyes.

Thank you to Mom, Rob, Cedar, and Tahlya, for your good humor, your love, and your support of every new project I take on. I'm lucky to spend my Ithaca days with you.

Over the 24 years I've lived in Ithaca, I've had the pleasure of getting to know so many brilliant people. I know that my privilege has afforded me the opportunity to participate in many things, with one door leading to another door, opening new insights into Ithaca that I'd never experienced before. I'm grateful for every one of those doors; the friendships, jobs, landscapes, events, gatherings, volunteering, trails, rallies, and projects have given me a wonderful and winding path to follow.

Thank you, Ithaca.

PREFACE

I came to the Finger Lakes on a whim in 2000 to work at Farm Sanctuary. I was a young traveler, floating from place to place, with an intention to move on when my season at the farm ended. But on days off, as I visited Ithaca, driving over the rolling autumn hills, dropping into the valley with the city and college lights sparkling, the landscape started to etch itself into me. With its lake and music and community and parks, Ithaca beckoned me to stay. And so, I did.

Some say that Ithaca is centrally isolated. Others say that Ithaca is 10 square miles surrounded by reality. I'd say both are true, and so much more. Ithaca is unique in that we have more than 100 waterfalls within those 10 square miles. We have an international airport, but no expressway. We have every amenity one needs, but it's more than an hour drive in any direction to the next largest city—Syracuse, Rochester, or Binghamton. We are significantly influenced by the three institutions of higher education anchored here—Cornell University, Ithaca College, and Tompkins Cortland Community College—and equally so by the rural, agricultural surroundings. Ithaca is a community of dreamers and idealists, striving for better in a world where dreams don't always come true. Our location, both physical and in our imaginations, defines who we are and who we will be.

The same could be said for individuals. Twenty-four years after I first arrived in Ithaca, I am grateful to have been shaped by this place. This book is a small way for me to celebrate the people and places that have inspired me and the things I find particularly wonderful about Ithaca. However, in a list of 100 things, there is no way to capture all the amazing artists, volunteers, activists, entrepreneurs, businesses, events, and icons of Ithaca. This book is by no means comprehensive.

Thanks to all our waterfalls, our tagline is "Ithaca is Gorges." The slogan has been wholly embraced and now the tagline is everywhere. Ithaca is love. Ithaca is books. Ithaca is cold. Ithaca is coffee. Ithaca is welcoming. Ithaca is, well, everything. I encourage you to discover for yourself what Ithaca is. You just might find that you decide to stay.

Shortstop Deli

FOOD AND DRINK

1

BREAK BREAD
AT ITHACA BAKERY AND COLLEGETOWN BAGELS

Are you looking for a chocolate regal cake for a birthday? Maybe you need a sourdough loaf for the family weekend at the lake. Or perhaps you're just glad to know that you can get a four-pound platter of cookies on any day of the week. For over 100 years, Ithaca Bakery has served the best bakery foods a hungry Ithacan might crave. A decade after serving its first bagel in 1976, the owners of Collegetown Bagels acquired and refurbished the Ithaca Bakery, joining the two esteemed eateries into one bagel-bakery-deli phenomenon. These days, you'll find the sister stores offering similar menus with distinctive sandwiches, homemade soups, exquisite desserts, and the finest breads. On weekends, the stores are always packed with locals and visitors. Weekday afternoons are a little quieter, and a great place to get some work done on your laptop or get a cuppa and croissant with a friend.

Ithaca Bakery
400 N Meadow St., 607-273-7110
2255 N Triphammer Rd., in Triphammer Marketplace, 607-257-2255
ithacabakery.com

Collegetown Bagels
420 College Ave., 607-273-0982
301 E State St., 607-273-2848
329 Pine Tree Rd., 607-273-1036
collegetownbagels.com

2

BE THE CAT'S MEOW

AT THE ALLEY CAT CAFE

Whether you're looking to adopt a new feline family member or want to sip your latte while watching kittens chase catnip mice, the Alley Cat Cafe is a cat lover's place to be. The café offers all the traditional coffee, tea, and espresso drinks (complete with names like Catpuccino and the Calico), using coffee beans from local Oak & Crow Coffee Co. The food side of the menu includes vegetarian sandwiches, salads, and baked goods, with many vegan options. The Alley Cat houses rescued cats and kittens from Browncoat Cat Rescue waiting to be adopted. A five-dollar fee—to help fund the care and feeding of the animals—gets you 30 minutes of cat time. The cats have the run of the secure and spacious cat rooms. Balls, string, tunnels, towers, and all manner of toys are available so you can adore the pouncing, purring, and playing kitties. Meow.

112 N Cayuga St., 607-319-5006, alleycatithaca.com

TIP

Browncoat Cat Rescue is a nonprofit that helps abandoned and mistreated cats in the Ithaca area. They maintain a foster care system, educate the community, and operate a Trap-Neuter-Return program to reduce the number of feral cats. For more than 10 years, they have successfully helped hundreds of cats find loving homes.

browncoatcatrescue.weebly.com

3

LA VIDA ES SUEÑO
AT ¡VIVA! TAQUERIA

With buoyant, colorful decor that matches the fresh, vibrant food, ¡Viva! isn't your typical Mexican restaurant. You'll find all the traditional dishes like tacos, enchiladas, and fajitas, but done with a healthy and unique ¡Viva! flourish. Whatever you order, you'd be wise to add a special side, like the Zesty Slaw or Queso Fundido cheese dip. The Escabeche—pickled carrots, garlic, onions, and jalapeños—takes every meal up a notch. There are plenty of vegetarian options, and many items can also be made vegan. The restaurant recently relocated and is now kitty-corner from its long time Restaurant Row location on Aurora Street. On the corner of the Commons, it now has a larger cantina, where there is more space to enjoy the specialty margaritas, tequilas, and sangria. Staying true to its beginnings as a counter-service taco and burrito shop, ¡Viva! allows you order ahead online for quick pickup at the takeout counter.

215 E State St., 607-277-1752, vivataqueria.com

TIP

Restaurant Row runs along Aurora Street, at the heart of Ithaca. There are many restaurants to choose from, so if one restaurant doesn't suit you, meander to the one next door. You're bound to find a favorite, whether Italian, American, or Pan-Asian. On warm days, the sidewalks are crowded with outside diners basking in the sun and talented waitstaff zipping to and fro.

4

GORGE YOURSELF
AT GORGERS

Banh mi. Caribbean Fire. Sweet Thai chili. Chimichurri. Cuban. These are just some of the sandwiches you'll find at Gorgers, a little sub shop that brings huge flavor to everything they make. The decade-old eatery was founded by two brothers who wanted to bring their take on globally-inspired, gourmet hot sandwiches to central New York. The team makes its own bread and sauces every day. Chicken, pork, and steak dominate the menu, but most subs can be made with fried eggplant or house-made seitan for a superb vegetarian option. All come with a pile of fresh veggies on top. The subs are the star of the show, but the salads, sides, and hand-cut fries are worth every bite. The tiny shop has a few tables inside, with a few more on the sidewalk, but it's just steps from the Commons where you can easily find a shady bench to gorge yourself silly.

116 W State St./Martin Luther King Jr. St., 607-319-5046
101 Main St., Cortland, 607-344-3229
gorgers.com

TIP

A note on street names: in an effort to enhance community inclusivity and awareness, the City of Ithaca dually named State Street as Martin Luther King Jr. Street. Businesses may use one or the other, or both of the names. Additionally, the Tompkins County Historical Commission installed signage along Cayuga Street in the language of the Gayogo̱hó:nǫʔ People, the Cayuga Nation, who are the original occupants of the Ithaca area.

5

EAT YOUR WAY AROUND THE WORLD IN COLLEGETOWN

Dozens of restaurants line the winding, hilly streets of Collegetown, ready to satiate your global cravings. The neighborhood grew out of its proximity to Cornell University as a walkable place for students and faculty to live and work. Since its inception in the late 1800s, the neighborhood's character and storefronts have evolved, always influenced by the university and its connection to downtown Ithaca. These days, the wide range of international students, professors, and residents who call Ithaca home have turned Collegetown into a hot spot of foodie flavor. You'll find sushi at a Japanese spot, dal at an Indian eatery, moussaka at the Greek place, and bibimbap at a Korean joint. Numerous restaurants offer pizza, wings, and burgers. If none of these suits your fancy, try a Mediterranean za'atar pie, Mexican tacos, or a Hawaiian poke bowl. Still not sure? Just head straight to dessert at one of the crêpe, cookie, or smoothie shops.

TIP

In summer months, the normal busy pace in Collegetown slows. Most students have left town, causing some restaurants to change their hours. Call ahead to confirm before heading to your chosen spot.

SOME OF THE COLLEGETOWN RESTAURANTS TO ENJOY

Souvlaki House
315 Eddy St., 607-273-1650

Sangam Indian Restaurant
424 Eddy St., 607-273-1006, sangamindianrestaurantithaca.com

Plum Tree Restaurant
113 Dryden Rd., 607-256-8212, goplumtree.com

Dos Amigos
403 College Ave., 607-379-5086, dosamigosfood.com

Luna Inspired Street Food
100 Dryden Rd., 607-256-5862, lunastreetfood.com

Chatty Cathy Cafe
327 Eddy St., 607-319-4176, chattycathycafe.com

TASTE THE TERROIR
OF THE FINGER LAKES ON THE CAYUGA LAKE WINE TRAIL

The special microclimate of the lakes and hills of the Finger Lakes makes the region a grape-growing wonderland. With the goal of promoting the region's affinity for viticulture, five wineries banded together in 1983 to create the Cayuga Lake Wine Trail. It was the nation's first organized wine trail and became a model for other regions. Now, there are a dozen wineries on the trail, celebrating and supporting community and agritourism. Each winery offers a unique experience, from small, rustic, boutique enterprises to vast estate operations with gift shops and cafés. Stop in to one for an afternoon wine tasting with a few friends, or spend several days meandering between all the wineries and discovering your favorite. Most of the wineries are pet friendly and kid friendly and have alcohol-free offerings. Many have picnic areas and offer outdoor seating to soak in the vineyard views while you taste.

cayugawinetrail.com

TIP

There are more wineries to visit all across the Finger Lakes. To the west of Cayuga Lake, the Seneca Lake Wine Trail includes nearly 28 wineries surrounding Seneca Lake. A little farther west, the Keuka Lake Wine Trail offers five wineries. Numerous other wineries dot the hillsides that are not affiliated with any of the wine trail organizations.

senecalakewine.com, keukawinetrail.com

7

LIFT YOUR MOOD
AT BOTANIST COFFEEHOUSE

A joint venture between coffee and plant lovers, Botanist Coffeehouse is one of Ithaca's newer, woman-owned, must-visit establishments. In the walkable neighborhood of Fall Creek, the atmosphere is warm, lush, and inviting, with greenery leafing out on the walls and shelves. Ithaca Flower Shop provides the variety of philodendrons, ferns, succulents, and other plants to adorn the shop. Many of the specialty plants are for sale, and Ithaca Flower Shop also offers custom floral bouquets and arrangements via their website. The Botanist's focus on nature creates a relaxing setting to sip your favorite coffee drink, of which there are many hot and iced options to choose. Coffee beans are from Coffee Mania, roasters in nearby Cortland. A rotating offering of daily pastries, including a cinnamon roll you won't want to miss, rounds out the experience.

1201 N Tioga St., 607-339-0088
botanistcoffeehouse.com, ithacaflowershop.com

8

GET THE BALL ROLLING
AT ATLAS BOWL

This isn't your grandpa's bowling alley! North of Ithaca in the quaint village of Trumansburg is Atlas Bowl, opened by Todd Parlato in 2015. This modern, eclectic venue is perfect for bowling a few games, relishing a chic dinner, meeting up with friends for a drink, or doing all three. There are seven lanes that can be reserved for parties or events. The menu favors quality over quantity and focuses on burgers and taco platters, with mouthwatering sides like fried brussels, crispy tofu, and totchos, a.k.a. tater tot nachos. Like many small businesses in the region, Atlas Bowl aims to use locally produced ingredients on its menu. The full-service bar offers cocktails, mocktails, and a range of beer and wine options. In 2023, Atlas Bowl expanded with the Back Alley, a comfortable outdoor patio and bar offering a creek-side view, additional seating, and fun games like cornhole.

61 W Main St., Trumansburg, 607-387-3191, atlasbowl.com

9

SPICE UP YOUR DAY

AT NEW DELHI DIAMOND'S RESTAURANT

There's lunch and then there's the all-you-can-eat lunch buffet at New Delhi Diamond's Restaurant. It's the best lunch deal in town. Fill your plate with samosas, rice, dal, curries, tikka masala, kebabs (and more!), and naan, raita, and chutney on the side. Diamond's has been offering flavorful food to the community since 1993, when the Sekhon family from Punjab, India, opened the restaurant in downtown Ithaca. Located just a block from the Commons, the atmosphere is humble, with a diner-like feel and the aroma of coriander, cumin, and cardamom in the air. Dinner is excellent too, with a menu covering the breadth of traditional, North Indian dishes. Diamond's also offers a small selection of wines and beers, including several Indian beers. Finish up with a mango lassi (milkshake) or mango kulfi (ice cream) to cut through the spice and make the meal perfectly delightful.

106 W Green St., 607-272-4508, newdelhidiamonds.com

10

GET THE SCOOP
AT CAYUGA LAKE CREAMERY

Cayuga Lake Creamery has been scooping their homemade ice cream since 2004. They offer about 30 flavors at a time from their list of 200 traditional, specialty, and seasonal options. If you're downtown, stop into their welcoming shop in Dewitt Mall for a cone. If you'd rather take a picturesque drive out of the city, head north on the Cayuga Lake Scenic Byway to Interlaken to visit the main creamery where the ice cream is made. The drive is doubly worth it because the creamery is also on the Cayuga Lake Wine Trail. This fact has resulted in a partnership with local wineries to create wine-flavored ice creams like King Ferry Winery Merlot Raspberry Sorbet, Lucas Vineyard Riesling Orange Sorbet, and Sheldrake Point Vineyard Summer Blush Chocolate Ice Cream. The Interlaken shop also offers sandwiches, soups, and sides if you're still hungry after your dessert.

215 N Cayuga St., in Dewitt Mall, 607-227-3987
8421 State Rte. 89, Interlaken, 607-532-9492
cayugalakecreamery.com

11

ENTER THE ENCHANTED BROCCOLI FOREST

AT MOOSEWOOD RESTAURANT

Who knew that when seven hippies got together in the 1970s to cook vegetables and share recipes they would change the face of the culinary world. But that's exactly what happened when Moosewood Restaurant opened in 1973. The Moosewood Collective, as it was known, was on the forefront of the organic movement and is recognized as one of the country's first and longest-operating vegetarian restaurants. Located on the first floor of historic Dewitt Mall, the restaurant underwent renovations in 2022, and is now under the management of the daughter of an original collective member. While early recipes were often heavy on dairy products, the rotating menu these days leans toward locally sourced and vegan ingredients in complex and sophisticated dishes. The bar offers New York beer and cider and Finger Lakes wines. Save room for a piece of vegan chocolate cake for dessert; it's absolutely enchanting.

215 N Cayuga St., in Dewitt Mall, 607-273-9610, moosewoodrestaurant.com

TIP

The original *Moosewood Cookbook*, published in 1974 by Mollie Katzen, has become one of the best-selling cookbooks of all time, with a dozen more cookbooks following in its wake. The restaurant has a shop where you can buy that classic along with many of the other titles.

12

HARVEST HEALTH AND HAPPINESS
AT INDIAN CREEK FARM

One of the wonderful things about Ithaca is that the city has all the culture and services you may need, but travel a few miles in any direction and you'll discover a beautiful agricultural landscape. Farms across the region produce unrivaled fruits and vegetables, and many open for U-pick activities in season so you can enjoy the fields yourself. Just north of the city, Indian Creek Farm grows many crops. Starting with strawberries in June, you can pick produce like summer peaches, peppers, and tomatoes, then autumn apples, pumpkins, brussels sprouts, and more. Stop at the farm store to grab your veggies if you don't have time for U-pick. Sign up for email crop alerts so you know the exact day when your favorites are ripe for the picking. Be warned: on fall weekends, the line for apple cider donuts circles the parking lot. But that cinnamon goodness is worth the wait.

1408 Trumansburg Rd., 607-227-8248, indiancreekithaca.com

OTHER U-PICK FARMS FOR FRUITS AND VEGGIES

Glenhaven Farm
Blueberries
6121 Sirrine Rd., Trumansburg, 607-387-9031, glenhavenfarm.com

Littletree Orchards
Apples and other tree fruits
345 Shaffer Rd., Newfield, 607-564-9246, littletree-orchards.com

Wickham's Tango Oaks Farm
Cherries, grapes, and tree fruits
5557 Rt. 414, Hector, 607-546-5511, facebook.com/tangooaks

Grisamore Farms
Strawberries, raspberries, and more
4069 Goose St., Locke, 315-497-1347, grisamorefarms.com

13

RUN AWAY TO THE CIRCUS TRUCK

FOR LUNCH

Authentic Italian homemade pasta dishes. Classic cheesesteak sandwiches. A TV from the 1980s playing old black-and-white VHS movies. Welcome to the Circus Truck! This hidden gem on Ithaca's west side is open weekdays until 2 p.m., year-round, rain or shine. Owner and chef J. P. has been serving up hot, tasty eats at the Circus Truck since 2009. This is a one-man operation, and every order is made fresh on the grill while you wait. Along with the daily lunch pasta specials, the menu also offers burgers, foot-long Coneys, and breakfast sandwiches, all with generous portions and killer flavors. The truck is tucked back in a parking lot off Green Street with a few picnic tables nearby. Note: call-ahead ordering saves wait time, and J. P. only takes cash. Once you discover the Circus Truck and have one bite of creamy alfredo or rich Bolognese, you'll be coming back every day for more.

720 W Green St., 607-229-5198, facebook.com/p/circus-truck-100083810568318

HIT A HOME RUN FOR FLAVOR

AT SHORTSTOP DELI

This deli's big glass windows and vivid orange and blue team colors aren't what make it stand out. Since 1978, Shortstop has been knocking it out of the park with their subs and sandwiches. Get right up to the counter in this busy deli to fill out a paper slip for your order. Start by choosing single, double, or grand slam size, then circle the bread, meats, veggies, and sauces you want. The lineup includes classics like turkey and cheese, pastrami, and tuna salad. For vegetarians, there's a tasty seitan option. Shortstop is also home base for Hot Trucks, a.k.a. "Poor Man's Pizza," purportedly the original inspiration for French bread-style pizzas. These toasted marinara, mozzarella, and pizza-topping subs are a late-night favorite among college students (and many hungry locals). There's no indoor seating, so be prepared to take your sandwich home or to a nearby park to dig in.

200 W Seneca St., 607-273-1030, shortstopdeli.com

TIP

When you buy any sub or sandwich, you can get a small/medium fountain drink for 10 cents, or a large drink for 29 cents. It's the best combo deal in town.

DEVOUR UNIQUE PUB FARE
AT RED'S PLACE

Located at the center of Aurora Street's Restaurant Row, Red's Place offers upscale pub food with panache. Entering Red's, you'll find a relaxed, comfortable atmosphere with simple decor that includes reclaimed barn wood, mason jars, and spacious booths. But the main thing you'll find is meals packed with flavor. From the Artisan Sandwiches list, the Farm to Ciabatta and Mushroom Lover's Melt are favorites. Choose from unique burgers like the Angry Pig (spicy pork sausage with cilantro-pesto aioli) or the PB & "Jellousy" burger (beef patty, cheddar, bacon, and peanut butter and jelly!). The drink menu offers local and regional beers and wines, as well as fresh takes on mixed drinks. There are also salads, appetizers, and flatbreads, with plenty of vegetarian, vegan, and gluten-free options. If you can't decide, just go with the soup of the day, which, no matter what it is, will be excellent.

107 N Aurora St., 607-319-4486, redsplaceithaca.com

OTHER GREAT PUBS

Northstar House
202 E Falls St., 607-216-8580, northstarpub.com

Ithaca Ale House
301 E State St., 607-256-7977, ithacaalehouse.com

The Corner Pub at Rogues Harbor
2079 E Shore Dr., Lansing, 607-533-0400, roguesharbor.com/dining

SATISFY YOUR SWEET TOOTH
AT DOLCE DELIGHT

Up on South Hill near Ithaca College, you'll find Dolce Delight, a bustling little corner café and bakery. Started in 2009 by Maria Cacciotti Salino, who runs the shop with her daughter, Dolce Delight offers all kinds of sweets and savories to brighten your day. There are a dozen types of breakfast sandwiches, pastries made fresh, a case full of cookies and chocolates, soups, salads, a rotating quiche of the day, and more. If this isn't enough, try the house specialty, the pie; from cherry to pumpkin to Salino's Pillsbury Pie Contest second-place winner, A Slice of Apple Spice. The shop also carries a few gifts and goodies from local makers. Order at the counter from the friendly staff and take your treats to the outdoor tables in warmer months. There are only a handful of tables inside, so get there early on winter weekends to claim your spot.

1080 Danby Rd., 607-272-0282, dolcedelightofithaca.com

TIP

Making quality food is a family affair for the Salino family. Next door to Dolce Delight is Italian Carry Out, operated by Maria Salino's sons. The pizzeria offers pizza, wings, pasta, meatballs, and more, often using traditional family recipes, which give their food that homemade goodness.
1070 Danby Rd., 607-256-1111, italiancarryoutithaca.com

17

GRAB A SLICE
AT FRANCO'S PIZZERIA

Sicilian brothers Franco and Salvatore Evola know how to make a pizza pie. Their New York–style pizza is faultless, but their Sicilian-style pies will make you feel like you're sitting on a hillside overlooking the Mediterranean Sea. Since they started serving on Ithaca's west end in 2017, Franco's has quickly become one of the most popular pizza joints in town, proven by its repeated wins for "Best Pizza in Ithaca" in the Ithaca Times annual reader poll. There are always fresh pies available to purchase by the slice, or order your favorites ahead for takeout. Also on the menu are calzones, strombolis, and garlic knots. In 2023, Franco's moved their location, but they didn't go far. Their new building across the street makes room for everyone with a larger space, more seating, and full accessibility.

527 W State St., 607-319-5132, francosithaca.com

OTHER LOCAL PIZZA FAVORITES

Sammy's Pizzeria
215 E State St., on the Commons, 607-203-0349
facebook.com/sammysithaca

Pizza Aroma
307 S Meadow St., 607-273-6165
facebook.com/pizzaaromaithaca

Eta Pie
1006 W Seneca St., 607-379-6066
etapie.com

New York Pizzeria
2 W Main St., Trumansburg, 607-387-3700

18

JOIN THE CRUST FUND
AT WIDE AWAKE BAKERY

The best thing since sliced bread is a slice of bread from Wide Awake Bakery. What makes this bread amazing is the care in each loaf. The organic grains are grown by local farm partners, milled at Farmer Ground Flour, an organic mill in Trumansburg, and baked in a wood-fired oven. Started by Stefan Senders, Wide Awake has been baking with community and sustainability in mind since 2010. Breads like sourdough, rye, pain au levain, and ciabatta can be purchased at the Ithaca Farmers Market and in regional stores. To become a part of the bakery community, join the Crust Fund and indicate how many loaves you want each week. Then stop at one of their pickup locations to get your weekly share. Lucky for Ithaca, in 2023, Wide Awake opened its own shop where you can pick up your favorite loaf, try a pastry, or sip an espresso.

435 Franklin St., wideawakebakery.com

MEET THE HERD
AT LIVELY RUN GOAT DAIRY

You may have done yoga before, but have you done goat yoga? In June and July, head to Lively Run Goat Dairy to get stretching and laughing on your yoga mat with a bunch of lively goat kids. Other fun activities at the farm include bottle feeding the baby goats in spring, feeding corn to the adult goats all summer; and in winter, enjoying the annual Christmas Tree Munch. If you prefer to appreciate the goats from afar, shop at the cheese and gift store, do a cheese tasting, or tour the farm and learn about cheese making. Family owned and operated, the dairy has been in business since 1982, making artisanal chèvre, feta, blue cheese, and more. While originally a goat dairy, Lively Run has also made cow cheeses such as gouda, brie, and cheddar for a decade. Lively Run products can be found at markets, wineries, and groceries around the state.

8978 County Rd. 142, Interlaken, 607-532-4647, livelyrun.com

20

EAT, DRINK, AND BE MERRY
AT LIQUID STATE BREWING COMPANY AND SILO FOOD TRUCK

Whether you're celebrating a birthday or the end of a long work week, Liquid State Brewing Company offers a cheerful gathering place to share craft beer with your buddies. The airy beer hall has long tables with plenty of room to squeeze in more friends. Large windows by the bar oversee the 17-barrel brewhouse and fermentation cellar where you can watch workers making those delicious brews. Beer types range from German and Belgian to IPAs and porters. Liquid State serves minimal snack foods, so fortunately, they've partnered with Silo Food Truck to offer amazing fare to pair with your drinks. Silo specializes in fried chicken and award-winning mac and cheese, but there are plenty other options from their menu of homestyle Southern cooking with a twist. The truck is stationed in the parking lot Wednesdays through Saturdays, and food can be enjoyed in the beer hall, on the outdoor patio, or for takeout.

620 W Green St.
liquidstatebeer.com, silofoodtruck.com

21

RELISH EACH BITE
AT TASTE OF THAI EXPRESS

While the name may connotate a fast-food joint, Taste of Thai Express is a full-service restaurant that has consistently delivered on flavor since 2003. Located on busy Meadow Street on Ithaca's west end, the restaurant's large windows allow for a sunny dining room experience. Taste of Thai Express uses locally made tofu from Ithaca Soy and uses as much local and organic produce as possible. The classic Thai dishes are organized into categories of "Yum" Thai salads, Thai-style fried rice, noodles, Asian wok stir-fry, and curries. The pad thai is unsurpassed. Try the massaman curry for a mild, sweet curry. If you're looking for serious spice, go for spicy basil stir-fry or green curry, or ask to add heat to any dish. Appetizers, soups, and Thai drinks complement the main course. A lunch menu and specials are served weekdays.

209 S Meadow St., 607-272-8424, tasteofthaiexpress.com

OTHER EXCELLENT THAI FOOD

Tamarind Thai Restaurant
503 N Meadow St., 607-277-2220, tamarindthaiithaca.com

Taste of Thai
216 E State St., on the Commons, 607-256-5487

Thai Basil
118 W State St., 607-319-4722, ithacathaibasil.com

DINE ON SURF AND TURF
AT THE BOATYARD GRILL

At the tip of Inlet Island, where Six Mile Creek meets the Inlet and flows into Cayuga Lake, you'll find the Boatyard Grill, a local favorite for seafood. Appropriately, the Boatyard is located on the waterfront next to the Finger Lakes Boating Center and Marina, and is bordered on two sides by water. The indoor seating has plenty of great views, but summer evenings on the deck, with live music playing and the cool breeze coming off the water, are picture perfect. The menu has many surf and turf favorites, from fried calamari and sizzling lobster to sirloin steak and the NY cheddar burger. The bar is stocked with local and imported beers and wines, as well as all the classic cocktails. If you just want to take in the view, mosey outside to the firepit and watch the wooden boats float past.

525 Old Taughannock Blvd., 607-256-2628, boatyardgrill.com

TIP

The Boatyard is often packed and they don't take reservations. They do have a "Phone Ahead Seating" policy: just call on the day you want to dine and you'll already be on the waiting list when you arrive. Easy peasy!

23

JUMP-START YOUR DAY
AT GIMME! COFFEE

Ithaca's coffee scene was forever changed when the first Gimme! Coffee shop opened in 2000. The retailer has expanded to five locations, and with several national awards and recognitions, Gimme! has proven itself as a high-quality specialty roaster. The beans are grown in places like Peru, Honduras, and Indonesia and roasted at the Gimme! facility in Ithaca. Sustainability is a key goal; most of their beans are organic and fair trade, and they build direct relationships with producers, such as the International Women's Coffee Alliance. All their careful efforts lead to superior flavor in your cup. Talented and friendly baristas serve your favorite drinks, from espressos to mochas to cappuccinos to flat whites. A small variety of baked goods and noncoffee drinks are available as well. The cafés offer a simple and modern atmosphere, and it's often hard to find a seat in these popular hangouts crowded with Gimme! devotees.

430 N Cayuga St., 607-277-8393
903 Hanshaw Rd., 607-391-0038
506 W State St., 607-272-8564
Gates Hall, Campus Rd., Cornell University campus, 607-227-5391
7 E Main St., Trumansburg, 607-387-3960
gimmecoffee.com

RAISE A GLASS
AT ITHACA BEER CO.

Flower Power. Apricot Wheat. CascaZilla. These are just a few of the flavorful and iconic beers you'll find brewing at Ithaca Beer Co. The company was founded in 1998, and, after outgrowing their original location south of the city, they built a large brewing and bottling facility where they now brew nearly 20,000 barrels of beer each year. All their drinks, including their tasty ginger and root beers, are distributed across the East Coast to 15 states. The taproom and restaurant opened in 2012 with a farm-to-table menu of sandwiches, burgers, wood-fired pizzas, and more. When the restaurant is booked, which is often, the outdoor beer garden has plenty of space to meet friends, grab a beer and snacks, and let the kids run free. Ithaca Beer opened a second taproom in Collegetown in 2022, making residents on East Hill very happy.

122 Ithaca Beer Dr., 607-273-0766
409 College Ave., Ste. A, 607-379-6197
ithacabeer.com

25

PUT A CHERRY ON TOP
AT PURITY ICE CREAM CO.

The vintage feel of Purity Ice Cream Co.'s ice cream parlor may take you back in time to the origin of the ice cream sundae. Though it's disputed by some, ice cream buffs know that on a Sunday in 1892, Ithaca pharmacy and soda fountain owner Chester Platt served a bowl of ice cream to Reverend John Scott. When he added cherry syrup and a cherry on top, he created a fabulous new treat that the men named a "Cherry Sunday." Since 1936, Purity has been dishing up their homemade ice cream, cupcakes, pies, doughnuts, and more. The lunch menu offers burgers, salads, and milkshakes. Purity has changed ownership a few times over the years, but it always remains dedicated to community involvement, quality ice cream, and excellent service. Go early to avoid the long evening lines filled with college students, little league teams, and everyone in Ithaca with a sweet tooth.

700 Cascadilla St., 607-272-1545, purityicecream.com

TIP

Sweet Melissa's Ice Cream Shop also serves up a scrumptious sundae, made with their homemade ice cream. The shop offers the best soft-serve in town. And with their central downtown location, Sweet Melissa's is a prime summertime hangout for ice cream lovers.

200 W Seneca St., 607-209-0070, sweetmelissasicecream.com

Boardman House

MUSIC AND ENTERTAINMENT

26

ROCK AND ROLL
AT THE CFCU DOWNTOWN ITHACA SUMMER CONCERT SERIES

One high point of life in Ithaca is spending a warm summer night jamming and dancing at the Downtown Ithaca Summer Concert Series sponsored by CFCU Community Credit Union and organized by the Downtown Ithaca Alliance. Every Thursday evening from 6 to 8 p.m., June through September, gather your friends and head over to the Bernie Milton Pavilion on the Commons. The summer lineup always includes a mix of favorite local bands as well as new musical acts playing everything from reggae to jazz to brass band to swing to hip-hop, and more. The concerts are great for the whole family and always free. There is plenty of space around the stage for folks to set up a lawn chair and tap their feet to the music or get down front and dance. A beer garden nearby offers beverages for concertgoers aged 21 and over.

Bernie Milton Pavilion, on the Commons
Downtown Ithaca Alliance
607-277-8679, downtownithaca.com/summer-concert-series

27

CATCH A RUNAWAY HIT
AT THE HANGAR THEATRE

The Hangar Theatre gets its name from its location in Cass Park on land once used as an airport by the Thomas-Morse Aviation Company throughout the early 1900s. One of the original plane hangars was converted into a seasonal stage, and the Ithaca Repertory Theatre—later renamed the Hangar Theatre Company—opened in 1975 with a production of *Man of La Mancha*. The Company only performed in the warmer months until a 2010 capital campaign raised funding to winterize the building. Now, the Hangar's Mainstage company performs shows year-round, from Broadway musicals like *Cabaret* and *Into the Woods* to dramas, adaptations, and plays. The Hangar also presents KIDDSTUFF, a summertime series that offers musicals, fairy tales, and performances that bring stories to life for young audiences. The concessions bar opens an hour before performances so you can mingle with other theatergoers or picnic on the patio before the show.

801 Taughannock Blvd., 607-273-2787, hangartheatre.org

PLAY IN THE STREET
AT STREETS ALIVE! ITHACA

Stop by a neighbor's lemonade stand. Get a henna tattoo. Join a jump rope contest. For one day each spring and fall, Streets Alive! Ithaca encourages folks to climb out of their cars and play in the streets. Streets Alive! started in 2012 when neighbors closed 10 blocks of Cayuga Street in the Fall Creek neighborhood and came out for a massive block party. Since then, the event moves to a different downtown neighborhood each time and welcomes all kinds of fun. You may come across bike repair stations, jugglers, chalk art, musicians, and more. Anything goes, from skateboarding to biking to in-line skating to just meandering and chatting with friends. Though volunteers make much of the event happen, Streets Alive! is hosted by Bike Walk Tompkins, an organization that works to promote the benefits of bicycling for fun, health, and transport.

607-301-3181, bikewalktompkins.org/streetsalive

TIP

As you enjoy Streets Alive!, keep an eye out for the Ithaca Physics Bus. This upcycled school bus is now a mobile science center bringing scientific experimentation and fun to the community. They hold activities outside the bus, but you can also climb aboard to try out a mix of eccentric and entertaining experiments.

freescienceworkshop.org/physicsbus

29

BE ENCHANTED
BY THE CAYUGA CHAMBER ORCHESTRA

Captivating performances, melodious sounds, and world-class conductors are the hallmarks of the Cayuga Chamber Orchestra, the official orchestra of the City of Ithaca. Founded in 1976, each season runs from September to June and features an array of concerts. You'll likely hear Beethoven, Haydn, Bach, and more in the orchestral series, performed at Ford Hall on the Ithaca College campus. The chamber series highlights a smaller ensemble and is performed at venues like the First Unitarian and First Presbyterian Churches. Part of the organization's mission is community education, exemplified by the family concert series, held in partnership with Tompkins County Public Library. These events include a concert and story time, after which kids can learn about and try the instruments. The youth orchestra offers children throughout the region the opportunity to participate and perform with a high-level symphony. No matter which event you attend, you're sure to be swept away by beautiful music.

607-273-8981, ccoithaca.org

BOB FOR APPLES
AT THE APPLE HARVEST FESTIVAL

When autumn arrives, that means apples. Crates of apples. And apple goodies galore: apple pie, candy apples, apple cider, apple cider doughnuts, and more. On one long weekend in September, apple growers, artists, food vendors, and musicians gather on the Ithaca Commons to celebrate the harvest season. The tradition of regional farmers coming downtown to distribute their apple produce began in 1982. The festival has grown and in recent years has incorporated games for kids, craft booths, a beer garden, and bands playing on stages around the city. Many local shops also get in on the fun with raffles and sales that add to an air of community levity. The Downtown Ithaca Alliance organizes the event, with the help of volunteers and numerous local sponsors. The Commons is always packed for this festival, rain or shine, so prepare to join the masses in your search for the sweetest apple variety.

Downtown Ithaca Alliance
607-277-8679, downtownithaca.com/apple-harvest-festival

TIP

Festivals revolving around food and drink are popular in Ithaca. The Downtown Ithaca Alliance also hosts the Chili Cook-Off in March. The Chowder Cook-Off in December takes things a step further and collaborates with the Ice and Lights Festival. This event showcases ice carving, a silent disco, and an ice bar—an outdoor bar carved out of ice and open for drinks on cold winter nights.

downtownithaca.com/events

31

CONNECT WITH THE BARD
AT THE ITHACA SHAKESPEARE COMPANY

All the world's a stage for the Ithaca Shakespeare Company, which brings the Bard's tragedies and comedies to life each summer. The Company grew from a group of thespian Cornell students, which, in 2001, began welcoming community members to their troupe. With their first production of *The Tempest* in 2002, a new company was born. It's foundation in outdoor performances—originally staged at Cornell Botanic Gardens, later at Cass Park, and then Robert Treman State Park—allows for the space for physical action and audience connection. The company performs one tragedy and one comedy each season and has staged classics such as *Macbeth*, *Romeo and Juliet*, and *A Midsummer Night's Dream*. Though some say that Shakespearean language is hard to understand—with their detailed costumes and sets, dynamic actors, and immersive performances, the Ithaca Shakespeare Company ensures that the joy of Shakespeare's work is accessible and loved by all who see the show.

ithacashakespeare.org

LET THE MUSIC MOVE YOU

WITH THE DOROTHY COTTON JUBILEE SINGERS

When you listen to the Dorothy Cotton Jubilee Singers, you'll wish the music would never end. Ithaca College professor Baruch Whitehead founded the group in 2010, wanting to preserve and sustain Negro spiritual music. The spirituals were created by slaves who, forbidden to read, passed on their traditions through storytelling and song. Singing a cappella, in four-part harmony, the DCJ Singers offer stirring performances throughout the year and at special events. The choir is named in honor of Dr. Dorothy Cotton, who worked alongside Dr. Martin Luther King Jr. for many years as the education director for the Southern Christian Leadership Conference. Dr. Cotton's work for the Civil Rights Movement spans decades and extends to her time in the Ithaca community and as director of student activities at Cornell University. Dr. Cotton was a skilled speaker and singer, and the Dorothy Cotton Jubilee Singers is a powerful tribute to her legacy.

dorothycottonjubileesingers.org

33

LIGHTS. CAMERA. ACTION!
AT CINEMAPOLIS

Cinemapolis has been bringing independent and international movies to downtown Ithaca since 1986. Originally a single screen in a basement below the Commons, the theater shows first-run films that you won't catch at traditional theaters (though some mainstream films make it onto the marquee). In 2009, the nonprofit organization mobilized extensive community support to expand to a larger location on Green Street to allow for stadium seating and five screens. The community also rallied in the early 2010s when Cinemapolis needed to upgrade to digital technology. The result is a cinema that people feel invested in and adore. In addition to arthouse films, Cinemapolis is an important venue for film festivals, locally produced film screenings, community presentations, and events. The concession stand has classic snacks and goodies, but it's the only theater in the region where you can get nutritional yeast on your popcorn—an all-time local favorite.

120 E Green St., 607-277-6115, cinemapolis.org

TIP

Ithaca has a history of being a movie-lover's town. In 1914, the Wharton brothers set up a movie studio in Renwick Park (now Stewart Park), bringing in famed screen stars of the time. The Whartons were on the cutting edge of the film industry and, over the five years they operated in Ithaca, made dozens of films. The Wharton Studio Museum is an up-and-coming nonprofit that works to preserve and share film history of the region.

whartonstudiomuseum.org

DANCE ALL NIGHT
AT GRASSROOTS FESTIVAL OF MUSIC AND DANCE

Four days. Four stages. Thousands of music lovers. Grassroots Festival showcases nearly 100 bands and musicians from as close as Trumansburg's Main Street to as far away as Ukraine or Democratic Republic of Congo. Each year you'll hear country, roots, orchestral, Cajun, folk, and more. The dance tent is always hopping with swing, contra, or zydeco dancing. Bands rock the stages late into the night, after which festivalgoers start up drum circles that last until dawn. The festival has plenty of kid-focused activities. Dozens of food vendors line the central grassy field, alongside vendors selling clothing, jewelry, and art. Originated in 1990 by members of the band Donna the Buffalo, Grassroots is a nonprofit organization with a handful of paid staff. However, in exchange for festival entry, hundreds of volunteers manage the setup, operations, safety, and cleanup of the event. The result is a celebration of community, generosity, and a shared love of music.

Trumansburg Fairgrounds
2150 Trumansburg Rd., Trumansburg, 607-387-5098, grassrootsfest.org

TIP

Buy tickets as a four-day package or for a single day. Ticket prices for ages 13 to 15 are reduced. Kids under 12 get in free with a guardian. Camping is available on-site or nearby off-site.

35

APPLAUD AN OUTSTANDING SHOW

AT THE STATE THEATRE OF ITHACA

A historical community asset like no other, the State Theatre will simultaneously take you back in time to the vaudeville era while also moving you forward to the future of entertainment. The 1,600-seat, two-story theater opened in 1928 and was a point of pride for the region. It ran vaudeville shows until the film era when it became primarily a cinema. The theater has undergone many renovations, but in 1998, Historic Ithaca (a nonprofit preservation organization) significantly updated and preserved the building. With its Moorish, Renaissance Revival, and Collegiate Gothic architecture styles, it's easy to see why the theater has been added to the National Register of Historic Places. The State hosts events from live concerts to community performances to stand-up comedians to movie screenings. While waiting for the show to start, look up at the blue ceiling; it's embedded with tiny LED lights that shower a magical atmosphere over everything.

107 W State St., 607-277-8283, stateofithaca.org

36

HEAR MUSIC IN THE AIR
AT PORCHFEST

Wander down Tioga Street during Porchfest and you might catch a musician singing the blues from someone's front porch. Head to Cayuga Street for an indie rock band. Turn the corner onto Yates Street and settle in to listen to a jazz ensemble. At this yearly event, a visit to the Fall Creek and Northside neighborhoods will surround you with talented musicians playing from house porches. The festival began in 2007 when Gretchen Hildreth and Lesley Greene brought together a couple dozen bands to play on friends' porches. The idea caught on and neighbors began offering up their porches. Now, Porchfest hosts nearly 150 bands and numerous food vendors, and in 2023, organizers added a Makers Market in a nearby park. The Ithaca Porchfest has inspired more than just locals. Nearly 170 neighborhoods around the US and Canada have followed the Ithaca model to host free, open-air, porch music in their communities.

porchfest.org

BE EN POINTE
WITH THE ITHACA BALLET COMPANY

Founded in 1961, the Ithaca Ballet Company brings graceful dance to audiences and students throughout the region. The company is upstate New York's only professional ballet repertory and performs productions throughout the year. It is the State Theatre of Ithaca's resident ballet company, but also performs at the Hangar Theatre and tours the Finger Lakes region. The company presents classical works, while also bringing contemporary ballets to the stage. The organization operates the Ballet Center of Ithaca, a school for dancers of all ages, whose alumni have gone on to professional companies around the country. Performing Tchaikovsky's classic *The Nutcracker* is the troupe's annual winter tradition, beloved by many Ithaca families. After an evening with this ballet, visions of sugar plums will surely be dancing in your head all night long.

607-319-0147, ithacaballet.org

38

SEE A POWERFUL FILM
AT THE FINGER LAKES ENVIRONMENTAL FILM FESTIVAL

Each spring, join students, artists, filmmakers, and educators at the Finger Lakes Environmental Film Festival. The festival started in 1997, and while each year's theme is different, it always explores issues of sustainability, cultural heritage, ecology, agriculture, housing, and many other topics related to living on planet Earth. Hosted by Ithaca College, the festival is a collaboration with Cinemapolis, Ithaca's downtown movie theater, which screens most of the films. You can see dozens of documentaries, full-length narrative works, and experimental films and screenings, and there is always a strong international focus to the films. Over the years, the festival has expanded both its schedule, now running for three weeks in March and April, as well as its breadth, which includes art and new media installations, concerts, panels, scholarly presentations, and more. You can pay to see each individual film, get a five-film pass, or buy a ticket giving access to every event.

ithaca.edu/finger-lakes-environmental-film-festival

39

GO BUG WILD
AT INSECTAPALOOZA

Want to get up close and personal with a honey bee hive? How about learn to identify butterfly species? Would you like to eat a cricket cookie? You'll have the chance to do all this and more at the Cornell Department of Entomology's Insectapalooza. This event is your only chance to see Cornell's impressive insect collection, which holds more than seven million insects from about 200,000 species and is generally closed to the public. Insectapalooza takes place in Stocking Hall, where you can move between classrooms to learn about your favorite insects, helpful pollinators, invasive pests, insect identification, biodiversity, and careers in entomology. The Entomology Department's goal is to educate kids and adults of all ages, while also inspiring appreciation for insects and having fun. Check out the Arthropod Zoo to see live specimens. You might even catch a cockroach race! Insectapalooza started in the early aughts, and this extremely popular event brings out thousands of bug lovers every year.

Stocking Hall, Cornell University campus
cals.cornell.edu/entomology/research-extension-outreach/insectapalooza

TIP

If you're in search of insect identification, send a sample to the Insect Diagnostic Lab, which will analyze your insect and send you information about it.

cuic.entomology.cornell.edu

40

SIT BACK AND ENJOY THE VIEW
AT SOUTH HILL CIDER

Take a break at South Hill Cider, where you can overlook a panoramic view of the Finger Lakes, relax with a cold drink, and listen to a local band jam some tunes. Founded in 2013 by musician Steve Selin, South Hill Cider produces specialty ciders made from their organic orchard apples as well as wild apples foraged from abandoned orchards. The food menu offers sandwiches, soups, and the quintessential cheese and charcuterie boards to pair with your cider, with ingredients sourced from regional farms and bakeries. Try new flavors and learn the details of cider making in the tasting room. On those long summer evenings, order your drinks and food, then head to the meadow to put your feet up in an Adirondack chair. Several nights a week, musicians play on the outdoor stage. It's an idyllic scene, perfect for an evening with friends or a family-friendly night out.

550 Sandbank Rd., 607-792-1097, southhillcider.com

OTHER VENUES FOR OUTDOOR MUSIC WITH A VIEW

Hopshire Farm and Brewery
1771 Dryden Rd., Freeville, 607-279-1243, hopshire.com

Finger Lakes Cider House
4017 Hickok Rd., Interlaken, 607-351-3313, fingerlakesciderhouse.com

Two Goats Brewing
5027 State Rte. 414, Burdett, 607-546-2337, twogoatsbrewing.com

41

DELIGHT IN PERFORMANCE ART

AT THE ITHACA COLLEGE SCHOOL OF MUSIC, THEATRE, AND DANCE

Whether you want to hear a jazz ensemble, African drumming, or a concert band, you'll find it at Ithaca College's School of Music, Theatre, and Dance. Ithaca College was founded in 1892 as the Ithaca Conservatory of Music, operating from the historic Boardman House downtown until moving to its South Hill campus in the 1960s. The school has one of the country's premier music programs and an equally impressive theater and dance program. The department offers faculty and student recitals, visiting musicians, orchestras, chorale concerts, musical theater, operas, plays, and more. There are also special performances for various holidays such as Veterans Day and Martin Luther King Jr. Day. All events are open to the public. Many concerts are free, but theater performances may have ticket charges. Find events listed on the college's calendar or sign up for newsletter updates.

Whalen Center and Dillingham Center, Ithaca College campus
ithaca.edu/academics/school-music-theatre-and-dance/music-concerts-and-events
ithaca.edu/center-theatre-and-dance-productions

TIP

Stop at the Dillingham Fountains, next to the Dillingham Center, for a stunning view over Ithaca and Cayuga Lake. The fountains have been an iconic campus scene since they were installed in 1966, and from spring through fall, they're lit up in various colors at night.

42

SPARK CONVERSATION
AT THE KITCHEN THEATRE

Founded in 1991, Kitchen Theatre Company is central New York's foremost venue to see off-Broadway plays. With their focus on experimental, bold, character-driven, provocative, and inclusive stories, they hold true to their slogan that "Important conversations happen in the Kitchen." The year-round company performs about a half dozen plays each year. Originally working from the historic Clinton House, in 2010, the Kitchen raised funds to build their intimate, 99-seat theater in a LEED-certified green building on State Street. There is no bad seat in the house with the actors up close and personal and audience members feeling like they are practically onstage. The Kitchen Sink series presents visiting artists and community events. The theater also hosts holiday and nonprofit fundraising events. Become a subscriber to ensure you have a seat at every performance.

417 W State St., 607-272-0570, kitchentheatre.org

EXPERIENCE THE ESSENCE OF ITHACA AT ITHACA FESTIVAL

Each June since 1977, Ithaca pulls out all the stops for its signature summer festival. It kicks off with Thursday night's parade, where you'll see folks from local organizations sporting kooky costumes alongside imaginative floats. Hula, belly, and ballet dancers shimmy by. Animal handlers with snakes, trained dogs, and horse-drawn carriages promenade past. Unicyclists, roboticists, and puppeteers fill the streets. Marchers may toss candy, but kids are equally likely to get handed a fresh carrot. All weekend, lineups of local musicians flood the Commons and surrounding venues with favorite tunes. One street is dedicated to food trucks serving every kind of cuisine you can imagine. Nearly 100 craft booths line another few blocks, where you can find your new favorite painter or potter or score some local honey. Each year the festival theme changes, so pick up a festival button or other swag to remind you to celebrate Ithaca all year round.

ithacafestival.org

TIP

There are many outstanding street performers at the festival, but you won't want to miss a show by Hilby the Skinny German Juggle Boy. Hilby travels the world with his act—a combination of outrageous circus stunts and sidesplitting comedy, often incorporating audience participation—but we're lucky that he always makes it home for the Ithaca Festival.

hilby.net

Cascadilla Gorge

SPORTS AND RECREATION

44

FIND SUMMERTIME REFRESHMENT
AT THE ALEX HALEY POOL

Alex Haley, the famed author of *Roots: The Saga of an American Family* and *The Autobiography of Malcolm X*, was born in Ithaca in 1921. Though Haley's family moved away when he was still an infant, Ithaca continues to celebrate his legacy, specifically with a municipal pool named in his honor. Operated by Greater Ithaca Activities Center, a division of the City of Ithaca, the pool is an oasis to beat the summertime heat in downtown Ithaca. Grab a spot under the trees to stash your gear before you jump in the cool water. Little ones can splash around in Max's Wading Pool. The entry fee is minimal and the pool is open throughout the summer. A large mural at the entrance was painted by Khalil Bey in 2015. It's a tribute to Haley's roots in Ithaca and reminds us all of the power of literature, art, and community.

408 N Albany St., 607-277-6169
cityofithaca.org/327/greater-ithaca-activities-center

TIP

Walk north a few blocks on Albany Street to Cascadilla Street to find a historic marker designating the house where Haley was born. In 1921, Haley's father was a graduate student at Cornell University and his mother was studying at the Ithaca Conservatory of Music (which later became Ithaca College). In remembrance of the Haley family, next to the house is a small, public park.

ROLL WITH IT
ON THE CAYUGA WATERFRONT TRAIL

The best way to get up close and personal to scenic Cayuga Lake is to spend some time on the Cayuga Waterfront Trail. The project began in the early aughts, and for nearly two decades various segments of the trail were added, updated, and completed, until all the pieces came together to complete the eight-mile, paved pathway. The trail winds along the lakeshore as it connects Ithaca's east side to its west, meandering through popular stops such as Stewart Park, Newman Golf Course, Ithaca Farmers Market, Ithaca Children's Garden, Allan Treman State Marine Park, and more. You'll find numerous benches, bike racks, and informational signs along the flat, accessible trail, accommodating all who want to walk, bike, roll, or otherwise appreciate the waterfront. The trail is also a certified Pollinator Pathway, which means it is landscaped with native plants for a pesticide-free and pollinator-friendly corridor.

friendsofstewartpark.org/cwthome

TIP

Newman Municipal Golf Course is a nine-hole course situated at the edge of the Cayuga Lake inlet. Operated by the City of Ithaca, the course has a pro shop, carts to rent, and beautiful views up to the hills surrounding Ithaca.

10 Pier Rd., 607-273-6262, newmangolfcourse.com

46

GET READY TO RUMBLE
AT ITHACA ROLLER DERBY

With a history dating back to the 1930s, Roller Derby has evolved into a full-contact sport with a punkish, campy vibe. In short, two tough-as-nails teams on roller skates try to score points by pushing past their opponents and circling the track. Players with cheeky derby names like Blucifer, Auntie Biotic, or Ziggy Skullcrush block their rivals, evade penalties, and elbow their way forward during each "jam," the short round of play within the period. The Ithaca League of Women Rollers was founded in 2008 with the SufferJets, named after the region's ties to suffragists and the women's rights movement. They later expanded to include a second team, the BlueStockings, as well as a junior league. The Ithaca League, a member of the Women's Flat Track Derby Association, holds bouts between their two teams and plays teams from other cities like Rochester and Philadelphia for a jamming, smashing, rocking fun time.

ithacarollerderby.com

FALL IN LOVE WITH NATURE
ON THE FINGER LAKES TRAIL

The Finger Lakes Trail rambles 580 miles across New York from Allegany State Park to the Catskill Forest Preserve. Seventy miles of the footpath passes through Tompkins County and Ithaca's southern end, through deep gorges, around evergreen forests, over creeks, and across fields of wildflowers. Several designated campsites and three-sided lean-tos dot the trail for hikers to spend the night or take a lunch break. The trail crosses state park and forest land, as well as private land easements, and is managed by the Finger Lakes Trail Conference. The trail is steep in some locations, but gentle and rolling in others, so be sure to check out the segment you plan to hike on the FLTC online interactive map or purchase waterproof paper maps from the online store. Locally, volunteers from the Cayuga Trails Club spend hundreds of hours maintaining and promoting the path to create a safe and pleasant hiking trail.

Finger Lakes Trail Conference Statewide Office
6111 Visitor Center Rd., Mt. Morris, 585-658-9320
fingerlakestrail.org, cayugatrailsclub.org

TIP

The highest point in Tompkins County is Connecticut Hill at 2,099 feet, marked by a radio tower off of Tower Road in Newfield. The FLT skirts this point but it is easily accessible from a short maintenance road. Though there is no view from the high point, the surrounding hardwood forest is a peaceful place for reflection.

BIRD-WATCH WITH THE BEST

AT THE CORNELL LAB OF ORNITHOLOGY

In 1915, Cornell University PhD student Arthur Allen advocated for a scientific laboratory and graduate program that specialized in living birds and their ecology. Cornell's Department of Ornithology was the first in the US and over its 100-plus-year history has become a global leader in the research, public education, and enjoyment of birds. The Lab of Ornithology grounds include five miles of trails on a 425-acre sanctuary known as Sapsucker Woods. These forests, ponds, and swamps are prime bird-watching territory. From indoors, the main building's wall of windows allows for observation of the pond habitats, and binoculars are available to use. Another indoor attraction is the Macaulay Library, the largest natural history sound and video archive of its kind. The visitor center and Wild Birds Unlimited store underwent renovations in 2023, with the new facilities to be unveiled in spring 2024. The new center will include expanded hands-on, art, and biology exhibits.

159 Sapsucker Woods Rd., 607-254-2473, birds.cornell.edu/home

TIP

The lab's All About Birds website helps with research on specific bird species, links to live bird cams, and offers online ornithology courses. Download Merlin, an app that will help you identify the birds you see and hear when you're outdoors.

allaboutbirds.org

GO WITH THE FLOW
THROUGH CASCADILLA GORGE

Just two blocks from the heart of downtown, you can enter Ithaca's most charming gorge. Follow the trail under bridges arching high above, alongside steep rock walls trickling water, and past at least six waterfalls and numerous smaller cascades. The cool, shady gorge is prime real estate for ferns, mosses, and a host of wildflowers. Starting at Linn Street, you'll climb about 400 feet over one-third of a mile. The upper portion of the trail continues along the creek and flattens out over another half mile. The stone pathways, staircases, and bridges were constructed in the 1920s, with stabilization and rebuilding projects completed in recent years. The Cascadilla Gorge Trail is maintained by Cornell Botanic Gardens. It's a popular tourist hike, as well as a commuter route for locals living downtown and working at Cornell University. What a beautiful way to get to work.

cornellbotanicgardens.org/location/cascadilla-gorge

TIP

Be careful at all the gorges and waterfalls throughout the region. Swimming is prohibited in most places and can be very dangerous. The ice-cold creek water can cause hypothermia even in warm months. Follow posted signs at all natural area locations. Cascadilla Gorge, like many area gorges, is closed during winter due to icy conditions.

50

CHEER FOR THE BIG RED
AT A CORNELL HOCKEY GAME

The Cornell men's hockey team played its first game in 1901, while the women's team formed in 1971. Today, both men's and women's teams play Division I athletics and have competed for national and regional championships in the NCAA, ECAC, and Ivy Leagues, with many wins under their belts. The men's games pack the house, including a rowdy student section with traditions of chanting at the opposing team. The women's games are great for families and those wanting to watch exceptional hockey without the roughing. In the past few decades, the women's team has produced numerous Olympians, with five Cornellian women playing in the 2022 Beijing Games. Many of the students on both teams are award-winning athletes and have moved on from the university into professional leagues. The games are high energy and exciting to watch, in part thanks to the pep band, which brings an irresistibly merry mood to each event.

Lynah Rink, 536 Campus Rd., Cornell University campus
cornellbigred.com/sports/womens-ice-hockey
cornellbigred.com/sports/mens-ice-hockey

51

TAKE A JAUNT
TO CASS PARK

Whether you want to circle the rink on skates, play softball with your buddies, or do some laps in the pool, Cass Park is the place to have fun while getting fit. The City of Ithaca purchased the flat, marshy lands on the west side in 1908, and when the Cayuga Lake inlet was dredged, the wetlands were filled in. The area was earmarked for a municipal park but was used in the early days of aviation by the Thomas-Morse Aviation Company, an airplane manufacturer that supplied planes for World War I. By the 1970s, the city had built a marina, ice rink, and Olympic-sized pool. Today, there are tennis courts, playing fields, playgrounds, and pavilions. The ice rink and pool are open seasonally. If you're looking to run, bike, or ski, one trailhead for the Black Diamond Trail begins here, and a portion of the Cayuga Waterfront Trail passes through as well.

701 Taughannock Blvd., 607-273-1090, casspark.org

TIP

Operated jointly with the Ithaca Youth Bureau, all the park's fields and facilities can be rented for sports events, parties, and games. Admission prices for the ice rink and pool are exceptionally low for residents of the City and Town of Ithaca, and only slightly higher for others. Since the 2020 pandemic, the rink requires preregistration for skaters.

FEEL THE ENERGY
OF ITHACA FALLS

Fall Creek originates about 33 miles to the northeast of Ithaca then meanders through Tompkins County, finally tumbling to its lowest level at Ithaca Falls. The water drops a massive 100 feet, across a 150-foot width, then flows on flat terrain into Cayuga Lake. The waterfall is a beautiful sight from Lake Street Bridge, but up close you'll really feel its intensity. Take the short but rocky trail into the gorge where you'll walk under towering sycamore trees as 400-million-year-old shale crumbles down the steep walls. Approaching the falls, the crashing water drowns out all sound and the cool spray of mist dampens everything. The power of the falls is exhilarating, but stay back from the water for safety. Swimming and wading are prohibited. In spring, summer, and fall this is a popular fishing spot. In winter, Ithaca Falls is often frozen in a gorgeous sheet of white ice.

On Lake Street near Falls Street intersection
ithacatrails.org/site/ithaca%20falls

TIP

Upstream along Fall Creek are several more impressive falls. Though there is no trail through the gorge and you can't get up close to the other falls, you can easily view and photograph them from the Stewart Avenue Bridge, University Avenue footbridge, and Beebe Dam Bridge.
cornellbotanicgardens.org/location/fall-creek-gorge

GO YOUR OWN PACE
ON THE BLACK DIAMOND TRAIL

The Lehigh Valley Railroad operated the Black Diamond Express beginning in 1896 and professed to be the fastest route from New York City to Buffalo. Service stopped in 1959, but you can still travel on the scenic, forested segment between Ithaca and Trumansburg by biking, walking, or skiing along the Black Diamond Trail. After decades of planning and construction, the rail trail was completed in the mid-2010s, thanks to collaboration between volunteers, town and city councils, and the New York State Parks Department. The stone-dust trail starts at Cass Park and rises for 8.4 miles along a gentle incline. Bridges over several waterfalls and creeks are a good place to catch your breath, and a half dozen road crossings with small parking areas offer the chance to tailor your trip length. Go onto the old railway bed at the Taughannock Falls State Park terminus for a stunning view over Upper Falls of Taughannock Creek.

parks.ny.gov/parks/blackdiamond

TIP

If you're looking for a tune-up or need a gear upgrade, head to Cayuga Ski & Cyclery before you hit the trail. Their experienced staff will help you find the right equipment, accessories, and clothing for your favorite bike and ski activities.

624 W State St., 607-277-6821, cayugaskiandcyclery.com

OTHER SCENIC RAIL TRAILS IN THE AREA

Dryden Rail Trail

This 14-mile, level trail runs from Dryden Lake to Freeville, with another section in the works from Freeville to Etna. The Varna section connects to the East Ithaca Recreation Way.

drydenrailtrail.org

East Ithaca Recreation Way

This multiuse rail trail offers 3.5 miles of trail and is a useful connector on the eastern hills through the Cornell University campus to the City of Ithaca.

ithacatrails.org/site/east%20ithaca%20recreation%20way

South Hill Recreation Way

This 3.5-mile rail trail extends across South Hill past Ithaca College. The trail also offers access points for walking trails into Six Mile Creek Natural Area.

ithacatrails.org/site/south%20hill%20recreation%20way

UNLEASH FUN
AT THE ITHACA DOG PARK

This isn't your typical city dog park! Situated with a beautiful view at the north end of Cass Park, the Ithaca Dog Park is more than an acre of running, roaming, and frolicking space for dogs of every stripe. While your dog plays, rest on one of the benches or stroll the gravel path. There's a water pump for filling bowls and summertime puppy pools, and a fenced area for small dogs. The park is funded by donations and the volunteer work of the Tompkins County Dog Owners Group. The NYS Office of Parks supports the dog waste compost system, which diverts about 7,000 pounds of waste from landfills. Owners are required to scoop their dog's poop and put it in the receptacles around the park. It's then converted into nutrient-rich organic material and used to enhance soils around New York parks—an excellent solution that keeps the park clean for everyone.

805 Taughannock Blvd.

55

HUG A TREE
AT THE CORNELL BOTANIC GARDENS

An herb garden with 500 varieties. Flowering trees blooming for weeks. Two hundred forty miles of footpaths and trails. The Cornell Botanic Gardens stewards these and 3,600 acres of natural areas. Stop by the Nevin Welcome Center for a map and to visit the winter garden, bioswale garden, rhododendron knoll, and other specialty gardens. The F. R. Newman Arboretum includes 150 acres of sustainably maintained meadows, a sculpture garden, a Holocaust memorial, several ponds, and numerous tree collections such as magnolia, beech, and oak. In addition to the gardens and arboretum, the botanic gardens maintains 22 unique landscapes across the region, including gorges, old-growth forests, and wildflower preserves. As a unit of Cornell University's College of Agriculture and Life Sciences, the botanic gardens also support student research and public education. Though some parking areas require payment, all gardens are open year-round and entry is free.

Nevin Welcome Center
124 Comstock Knoll Dr., 607-255-2400, cornellbotanicgardens.org

ADVENTURE ON THE WATER
ALONG THE CAYUGA LAKE BLUEWAY TRAIL

Glacially formed 10,000 years ago, Cayuga Lake is 435 feet deep, 3.5 miles wide, and, at 40 miles long, the longest of the 11 Finger Lakes. But the lake is more than just numbers, and getting offshore offers the chance to truly understand the grandeur of the Cayuga Lake Basin. Because much of the shoreline is privately owned, in the early 2010s, several communities that border the lake began a project to create a public water recreation trail to offer improved access. Now, Cayuga Lake Scenic Byway, Inc., a nonprofit dedicated to enhancing the Cayuga Lake region, oversees and promotes the Blueway Trail. They produce a waterproof pocket guide and map for nonmotorized paddle craft, detailing launch points, suggested paddling routes, and towns to stop in alongside the lake. From the Erie Canal locks in the north to the weeping willows at Stewart Park in the south, there is much to explore on the water.

cayugalake.com/cayuga-lake-blueway-trail

TIP

If you don't have your own canoe, kayak, or stand-up paddleboard, rent one from Paddle-N-More, or sign up for one of their guided water tours or paddling lessons. They have three locations around the lake and are open in season from Memorial Day through Labor Day.

607-288-3470, paddlenmore.com

57

BE HAPPY AS A PIG IN CLOVER
AT FARM SANCTUARY

If you love animals, venture to Farm Sanctuary, a 45-minute drive west of Ithaca, near Watkins Glen. Farm Sanctuary is a scenic and exceptional place that provides 275 acres of serene meadows as a safe haven for farm animals. The sanctuary was founded in 1986 as a place to take in abused animals. More than 500 animals inhabit the farm, from chickens to pigs to sheep, all of whom came from factory farms or neglectful owners. To meet some of the rescued residents, sign up for a farm tour, which lasts about an hour. The farm also hosts a Thanksgiving Celebration *for* the Turkeys, including a vegetable feast presented to the turkeys, to encourage people to appreciate, and not eat, turkeys during the holiday season of gratitude. If you want to support your favorite goat or cow, read some of their stories online and "adopt" the animal to help pay for its care.

3136 Aikens Rd., Watkins Glen, 607-583-2225, farmsanctuary.org

TIP

Farm Sanctuary advocates for a vegan diet as a healthy, environmentally sound, and compassionate lifestyle. Ithaca's Angelhearts Diner is an entirely vegan restaurant that serves up comfort diner-style food like stacks of soy buttermilk pancakes and tofu scramble breakfast burritos. The Philly "cheesesteak," made from seitan and cashew cheese, is unmatched. Oak & Crow Coffee Co. runs a coffee bar at the diner as well.

401 E State St., Ste. G2, 607-319-4205
angelheartsdiner.com, oakandcrow.com

DIG INTO GEOLOGY
IN THE NEW YORK STATE PARK GORGES

Ithaca gets its iconic slogan "Ithaca is Gorges" for good reason. There are no less than 100 waterfalls within 10 square miles of Ithaca, most of which cut through steep gorges. These gorges were formed over thousands of years as glaciers pushed into the landscape and carved the weak, unstable sedimentary rock. When the glaciers receded, they left cavernous gouges, called hanging valleys, and opened the way for flowing water to cause erosion and create waterfalls. There are many off-the-beaten-path falls, but Buttermilk Falls, Robert Treman, and Watkins Glen state parks are excellent places in and near Ithaca to access the gorges. All three parks have stunning trails where you'll climb old stone staircases, see dozens of waterfalls, and meander on curving pathways through geological wonders. In the summer, Buttermilk and Treman offer two of the few locations where you can legally and safely swim right at the base of the falls.

Buttermilk Falls State Park
112 E Buttermilk Falls Rd., 607-273-5761, parks.ny.gov/parks/buttermilkfalls

Robert Treman State Park
105 Enfield Falls Rd., 607-273-3440, parks.ny.gov/parks/roberttreman

Watkins Glen State Park
1009 N Franklin St., Watkins Glen, 607-535-4511, parks.ny.gov/parks/watkinsglen

TIP

If you plan to visit numerous state parks or visit on multiple days, consider buying the New York State Empire Pass, which covers the entrance fee for all New York state parks for the whole season. Additionally, NYS Parks will honor the National Park Service's Every-Kid-in-a-Park Pass, offering fourth graders and their families free entry into any park.

59

CATCH A WHIFF OF THE CORPSE FLOWER

AT LIBERTY HYDE BAILEY CONSERVATORY

Though the scent of rotting meat is not generally one that people take pleasure in, smelling the odor of a corpse flower at Cornell University's Liberty Hyde Bailey Conservatory is a singular experience. The corpse flower, aka titan arum, is an endangered rainforest plant native to Sumatra, Indonesia, that can reach nine feet tall. Its strategy for attracting pollinators is to emit the putrid aroma of decaying flesh. The conservatory maintains two titan arum plants, named Wee Stinky and Carolus. Blooms happen every seven to 10 years and last for about 48 hours, making one sniff an extraordinary event. Fortunately, scientists have coaxed these wonderfully weird flowers to bloom more often, and there are plenty of other plants to enjoy in the meantime. The conservatory's collection includes more than 650 species of cacti, orchids, carnivorous plants, and one of the world's largest palm collections. Follow the conservatory's Instagram or get email updates to find out when plants are blooming.

236 Tower Rd., Cornell University campus, conservatory.cals.cornell.edu

TIP

When you've had your fill of stinky smells and botanical beauties, head down the street to the Cornell Dairy Bar, where you'll only find sweetness. The main scoop here is Cornell Dairy ice cream, but you can grab a bagel, baked goods, or coffee as well. Though the corpse flowers bloom rarely, the Dairy Bar is open most days of the week. Check their website for current hours.

Stocking Hall, 411 Tower Rd., Cornell University campus
607-255-7660, scl.cornell.edu/cornell-dairy-bar

ENJOY A PICNIC
WITH A VIEW AT STEWART PARK

Every great city needs a great park, and Ithaca's Stewart Park surpasses the best. The park, which was added to the National Register of Historic Places in 2023, sits at the southern end of Cayuga Lake, offering an astonishing vista of green hills rising from miles of blue water. The location was originally a Cayuga Nation village. After colonization, the area was privately owned by the wealthy Renwick family. In 1921, Mayor Edwin Stewart championed revitalizing the park for public use. When Stewart died a month before the park's opening, the city named it after him. In its long history, the park has housed a zoo, a school, a vaudeville theater, and a movie studio. With its old willow trees lining the shore, the park is a scenic location for picnicking and playing, with tennis courts, an accessible playground, a carousel, and pavilions. The park hosts festivals, employee picnics, summer camps, and friendly sports gatherings.

1 James L. Gibbs Dr.
cityofithaca.org/516/stewart-park, friendsofstewartpark.org

TIP

The Cayuga Lake Basin is a prime birding environment. The area within Stewart Park known as the Fuertes Bird Sanctuary includes 55 acres of fully forested bird habitat. The Cayuga Bird Club maintains the sanctuary area.
cayugabirdclub.org

61

GET AWAY FROM IT ALL
IN THE FINGER LAKES NATIONAL FOREST

As you drive west from Ithaca, take in the picturesque rolling hills and broad views that typify the region. Just 20 minutes away, on a ridge between the two largest Finger Lakes, is the Finger Lakes National Forest, the only national forest in New York State. The forest comprises approximately 16,000 acres of piney woodland, steep ravines, and blue ponds. Designated as multiuse, some of the land is used as pasture, which creates an important grassland habitat. About 30 miles of trails cross the region for nature lovers to hike, ski, horseback ride, and bike. Designated camping areas for horseback riders, large groups, and hikers are busy in the summer but open up in the shoulder seasons. Foster Pond and Potomac Ponds can be accessed off Potomac Road and are excellent locations for fishing, swimming, and bird-watching. If you need an escape from city life, start here.

Hector Ranger Station
5218 State Rte. 414, Hector, 607-546-4470, fs.usda.gov/main/gmfl/about-forest

CRUISE THE WATERWAYS
WITH DISCOVER CAYUGA LAKE

If you want an awe-inspiring perspective on Ithaca, climb aboard the MV Teal for a tour around Cayuga Lake. The Teal is a 63-foot tour boat that can hold up to 70 passengers, operated by Discover Cayuga Lake. Take an ecotour, a sunset cruise, or a family cruise. You can bring your own snacks and drinks if you want to picnic during the ride. One of Discover Cayuga Lakes's goals is to provide education and a deeper understanding of the lake. They work with community partners to promote sustainability and environmental literacy and offer citizen scientist lake-monitoring cruises, as well as Floating Classroom cruises for students to learn about environmental and watershed sciences. Discover Cayuga Lake also offers one-hour tours departing from the Ithaca Farmers Market on Saturdays and Sundays during market season. Reservations are not required for the market tours, but highly recommended for all other cruises.

1000 Allan H. Treman Marina Rd., 607-327-5253, discovercayugalake.org

TIP

If you're looking to dock or launch your own boat, you can do so at Allan H. Treman State Marine Park (not to be confused with Robert Treman State Park). In addition to the seasonal boat slips, there is an eight-lane launch ramp and various day-use facilities.
805 Taughannock Blvd., 607-272-1460, parks.ny.gov/parks/allantreman

63

WHILE AWAY THE DAY
AT TAUGHANNOCK FALLS STATE PARK

At 215 feet, Taughannock Falls (pronounced tuh-GAN-nick) is the tallest waterfall east of the Mississippi. From Taughannock Boulevard, a flat, one-mile trail follows Taughannock Creek through the gorge to a viewing area at the base of the falls. Water plummeting down the side of the enormous, erosion-carved bowl is awe inspiring. For more challenging hikes, both the North Rim and South Rim Trails have significant elevation gain. While the falls is a highlight, you can easily spend a whole day relaxing by Cayuga Lake, making the most of everything the park has to offer. A large playground, guarded swimming area, and seasonal concession stand will keep the kids busy. Picnic tables and grills dot the grassy peninsula that juts into Cayuga Lake. A boat launch is available for paddle craft and motorboats. Check out North Point for an area that is less bustling and perfect for sunbathers, Frisbee players, and loungers.

1740 Taughannock Blvd., Trumansburg, 607-387-6739
parks.ny.gov/parks/taughannockfalls

TIP

If you only have time for a quick stop at Taughannock, the Falls Overlook on Taughannock Park Road is a spectacular place to view and photograph the entire waterfall bowl. You'll find a visitor center there for maps, information, and "Ithaca is Gorges" gear.

JUMP IN THE MUD
AT THE ITHACA CHILDREN'S GARDEN

Studies show that nature play and outdoor immersion are critical for children's independence, development, and well-being. This is the vision behind the Ithaca Children's Garden. Arriving at the ICG, you'll be greeted by Gaia the Giant Turtle, a large, climbable land sculpture and a good introduction to the garden's natural play spaces. Kids (and their caregivers) can clamber through a troll house, catch frogs in the rice-paddy pond, or meander along the story walk. A particularly popular area of ICG is the Anarchy Zone, where kids are encouraged to climb trees, build forts, and dig for worms. All seasons are magical, but ICG bursts to life in spring as thousands of flowers bloom in the wildflower meadow, bird garden, and the Bulb Labyrinth Memorial Garden. No visit to ICG is complete without sampling herbs from the kitchen garden and discovering the overgrown pathways between the garden areas.

121 Turtle Ln., 607-319-4203, ithacachildrensgarden.org

TIP

International Mud Day began in 2009 when folks from the World Forum Foundation in Nepal talked with peers in Australia about why their kids were unable to or discouraged from playing in the mud. The communities collaborated and now the day is celebrated each June around the world. ICG celebrates the ecological importance and great fun of mud with an all-day event including digging mud slides, crafting mud paintings, building mud pies, and more.

ithacachildrensgarden.org/portfolio/mud-day

A. D. White Library

CULTURE AND HISTORY

LET YOUR IMAGINATION RUN WILD
AT THE SCIENCENTER

The Sciencenter is more than just a hands-on science museum; it's a place where community comes together to explore the scientific world. Founded in 1983 by local educators who knew the value of teaching science to youth, the Sciencenter grew from an enthusiastic community with the support of science greats such as Carl Sagan and Bill Nye. The Sciencenter draws visitors from throughout the region with its hundreds of exhibits that encourage play and experimentation and bring astronomy, engineering, sustainability, hydrology, meteorology, and physics to life. Programs and events are presented throughout the year, and the Curiosity Corner allows children under age 4 to explore in an age-appropriate environment. The live animal exhibit shows snakes, frogs, and fish, and the Tidepool Touch Tank lets visitors get to know saltwater creatures. Outdoors is a seasonal mini golf course and an accessible, science-focused playground.

601 1st St., 607-272-0600, sciencenter.org

TIP

When you enter the museum, you can't miss the clickety-clack of the two-story ball machine. Titled *Quantum's Last Leap*, the autokinetic sculpture was built by George Rhoads and is one of hundreds of ball machines around the world. Try to follow a single ball through the maze or just stand back and marvel at the magic in this machine.

66

SHOW YOUR TRUE COLORS
DURING ITHACA PRIDE MONTH

Rainbows abound in Ithaca to celebrate June LGBTQ+ Pride Month with stores, restaurants, and local governments flying the Pride flag from their windows and flagpoles. Each year's activities are slightly different as local organizers work in conjunction with the Downtown Ithaca Alliance to put together a fun slate of events. The rain-or-shine pedestrian Pride Parade through downtown is followed by a dance party on the Commons. The Tompkins County Public Library hosts a book club, family story time, writing workshops, and discussion groups. Bars offer open mic nights, bingo, and happy hours, while local theaters present films and events. A variety of drag shows round out the lineup. Pride is more than a month of activities, and the diverse Ithaca community is always striving for more equity. Throughout the year, many businesses display an "Ithaca is Inclusive" sign to indicate that they welcome LGBTQ+ people and their families.

Downtown Ithaca Alliance
607-277-8679, downtownithaca.com/pride

GET TO KNOW LOCAL HISTORY

AT THE NEWFIELD COVERED BRIDGE

Passing through the oldest covered bridge still in use in New York State, you can imagine the clip-clop of horse hooves and the rattle of the carriage on the wooden planks. The bridge was built in 1853 in the rural hamlet of Newfield, a 15-minute drive from the city of Ithaca, to span 115 feet across the west branch of Cayuga Inlet. When visiting, notice the bridge's Town lattice truss style of construction that exhibits an intricate crisscross of beams popular at the time of building. Though the bridge has been renovated, repaired, and updated a few times over the years, the sturdy construction has proven it can stand the test of time. The Newfield Historical Society maintains historic records and images of the bridge. In any season, the covered bridge is a photogenic backdrop for family photos, but the colors of autumn make for truly remarkable scenery.

20 Bridge St., Newfield, newfieldhistoricalsociety.org/html/bridge.html

TIP

After visiting the bridge, stop next door at the Covered Bridge Market and Pizzeria for a soda, sandwich, hot soup, or a slice. The friendly eatery is a favorite for locals and visitors alike.

176 Main St., Newfield, 607-564-9901
facebook.com/p/covered-bridge-market-pizzeria-100047782939380

68

MARVEL
AT THE MAGNIFICENT A. D. WHITE LIBRARY

Architectural Digest included the A. D. White Library on its list of "26 Stunning University Libraries Around the World You Need to See," and when you walk in, you'll know why. You may think you've entered a fairy tale or been transported to a magical castle. The three-story, open-framework library is beautifully designed with wrought-iron scrollwork, upper-level balconies and walkways, and spiral staircases. Cozy nooks on every level offer study space for students. Famed local architect William Henry Miller, who was Cornell's first architecture student, designed the library. It was built in 1891 and honors Andrew Dickson White, one of Cornell University's founders and its first president. The library originally housed White's collection of more than 30,000 books; however, most of that collection has been moved to Cornell's rare book archives. There are still plenty of books to pluck off the shelves, so settle in and soak up the captivating atmosphere.

161 Ho Plaza, Cornell University campus, 607-255-4144
exhibits.library.cornell.edu/a-d-white-library-tour

69

MAKE AN EXCURSION
TO THE WOMEN'S RIGHTS NATIONAL HISTORICAL PARK IN SENECA FALLS

Though the struggle for women's rights continues to this day, drive just an hour north from Ithaca and you can visit the historic town where the movement was born. On July 19, 1848, suffragists Elizabeth Cady Stanton, Lucretia Mott, and Mary Ann M'Clintock led the first women's rights convention. This was the first public meeting held to specifically address freedom for women, and it led to more conventions and grassroots action for the suffrage and abolitionism movements. The convention included the reading of the Declaration of Sentiments, a proclamation that described the inequalities and failings of the contemporary laws and systems and declared women equal to men. Start at the national park visitor center where you can hear stories and perspectives and view documents and artifacts. Then tour some of the women's preserved homes, Declaration Park, and the Wesleyan Chapel, where the convention was held. Park entrance is free.

136 Fall St., Seneca Falls, 315-568-0024, nps.gov/wori/index.htm

TIP

Each July, the national park and local organizations host Convention Days, an annual commemoration of the first women's rights convention. The celebratory event includes speakers, workshops, art, music, and more.

SUPPORT LOCAL ARTISTS
ON THE GREATER ITHACA ART TRAIL

Have an eye for art? Love to discover new artists? With 55 talented artists on the Greater Ithaca Art Trail, you are bound to find a few gems to adorn your home. Across Tompkins County, local artists are creating a vast range of works like pottery, stained glass, jewelry, photography, fiber art, digital art, watercolor, and more. On the second Saturday of each month, artists participating in the Art Trail welcome visitors into their studios to share their art and their process. Most artists also participate in two exclusive October open studio weekends. To fill your art cravings, spend an autumn day exploring the county and stopping at different studios. A detailed map is available online and in many shops and galleries throughout Ithaca. If you can't make it out to the studio, most artists have online shops where you can peruse their work and order online.

Community Arts Partnership
607-273-5072, arttrail.com

71

FURTHER THE CAUSE OF FREEDOM

AT ST. JAMES A.M.E. ZION CHURCH

The African Methodist Episcopal Zion Church was incorporated in 1801, and the denomination has always been a leader in the struggle for Black people's freedom and equality. The humble St. James A.M.E. Zion Church on the south side of Ithaca played a central role in that struggle. Built in 1833 and recognized as Ithaca's oldest church building, St. James was an important stop on the Underground Railroad. The congregation and community upheld antislavery views and assisted many slaves as they escaped to the north. Leaders of the Underground Railroad such as Harriet Tubman and Frederick Douglass visited and spoke at the church, and Jermain Loguen, the "Underground Railroad King," served as the church's third minister. The St. James congregation remains dedicated to creating community, empowerment, and equity for all. Visit the church for Sunday services or special events, stop by to read the historical plaques, or request a tour of the building.

116 Cleveland Ave., 607-319-4249, stjamesithaca.com

UNCOVER ITHACA'S PAST
AT THE HISTORY CENTER

The Dewitt Historical Society was formed in 1935 to conduct local history research and collect and preserve documents. As the society grew, it shuffled to various locations, including to the county courthouse and historic Clinton House. By the 1970s, it expanded its focus to the entirety of Tompkins County and later renamed itself the History Center in Tompkins County. In 1994, the society opened a museum on Ithaca's east side. The organization moved to a brand-new location inside the Tompkins Center for History and Culture in 2019, which has permanent space for its research library and archives, exhibits, and educational programming. Meander the museum and listen to oral histories in the Story Vault, see the 1918 Tommy Plane (built in Ithaca by the Thomas-Morse Aviation Company, and, after 14 years of restoration, was flown across Ithaca in 2018), or purchase one of the many detailed history books about Tompkins County.

110 N Tioga St., on the Commons, 607-273-8284, thehistorycenter.net

TIP

The History Center offers a small number of tours such as the October Haunted History tour. They've collaborated with Historic Ithaca to create a variety of Pocket Sights self-guided walking tours. Pocket Sights tours can be downloaded to any phone and are free.

thehistorycenter.net/tours, historicithaca.org

KEY SITES TO SEE ON THE SELF-GUIDED DOWNTOWN HISTORICAL ARCHITECTURE TOUR

Boardman House
This 1866 Italianate-style house was used by the Ithaca Conservatory of Music (now Ithaca College) as one of its original campus buildings.
120 E Buffalo St., historicithaca.org/post/boardman-house

Tompkins County Old Courthouse
Built in 1854, this is the oldest Gothic Revival-style building in New York State. It is now the chambers of the Tompkins County Legislature.
121 E Court St., 607-274-5434, tompkinscountyny.gov/legislature

William Henry Miller Inn
A Queen Anne Victorian home designed in 1880 by local architect William Henry Miller. It now operates as a bed-and-breakfast.
303 N Aurora St., 607-256-4553, millerinn.com

Clinton House
This building was built in 1830 in the Greek Revival style to be used as a grand hotel and is known for its prominent columns. It was significantly renovated in 1872 and 1901, then fully restored in 1973. It is now used for offices and a charter school.
116 N Cayuga St., historicithaca.org/post/clinton-house

APPRECIATE ARTISTIC VISION

AT SALTONSTALL FOUNDATION FOR THE ARTS

The Constance Saltonstall Foundation for the Arts was founded as a nonprofit in 1995 to honor the legacy of Constance Saltonstall, an Ithaca painter, photographer, and historic preservationist. The 200-acre property of rolling hills and vast meadows in Ellis Hollow where Constance built her home was turned into an art colony upon her death. Throughout summer and fall, New York State artists, writers, and photographers convene at the Saltonstall colony and are offered the gift of time and space to focus on their craft. After each residency, the artists present exhibits and readings of their work. These open-house events are an excellent opportunity for the community to talk with the artists and enjoy what they've created. Walking in the summertime fields, coming together with fellow art lovers, and seeing and hearing innovative art and literature is truly inspirational.

435 Ellis Hollow Creek Rd., 607-539-3146, saltonstall.org

74

MEET YOUR MUSE
AT THE JOHNSON MUSEUM OF ART AT CORNELL UNIVERSITY

Situated high up on East Hill, the Herbert F. Johnson Museum of Art is a beacon of artistic excellence. The modern building was designed by I. M. Pei and houses an extensive permanent collection, which includes pre-Columbian, European, and South American art, to name a few. There are always rotating exhibits, which may include modern art, photography, or new media installations. A particularly captivating display is Leo Villareal's changing LED light installation titled *Cosmos*. Lay back on the zero-gravity bench in the second-floor outdoor sculpture court and let thousands of pinpoints of light mesmerize you. Don't miss the fifth floor, which houses the permanent Asian art collection. Each of the four outer walls on this floor is made of glass, offering a 360-degree, panoramic overview over Ithaca, Cayuga Lake, and Cornell University. It's the most spectacular view you'll find in the region.

114 Central Ave., Cornell University campus, 607-255-6464
museum.cornell.edu

SEEK PEACE
AT NAMGYAL MONASTERY INSTITUTE OF BUDDHIST STUDIES

In 1992, in a small, colorful house on Aurora Street, a handful of Tibetan monks opened the Namgyal Monastery Institute of Buddhist Studies, the North American seat of His Holiness the 14th Dalai Lama's Monastery. As a branch of the monastery in Dharamshala, India, their goal was to promote unity and peace and offer Americans a Tibetan Buddhism education program in a monastic setting. The monastery expanded to a large, wooded site on South Hill in 2004 where they built residences, classrooms, and retreat space. Then, in 2023, the institute opened the one-of-a-kind His Holiness Library, Learning Center, and Museum to house the works and teachings of the 14th Dalai Lama. When you visit, don't miss the Great Hall, a spectacular room with aspects of traditional Tibetan architecture and hand-painted and decorated walls and columns. The center offers classes and events, provides education for people of all faiths, and preserves and shares Tibetan culture.

201 Tibet Dr., 607-272-2785
namgyal.org, hhdalailamalibrarylearningcenter.org

76

INVESTIGATE THE NATURAL WORLD
AT THE CAYUGA NATURE CENTER

Founded in 1981, the Cayuga Nature Center's goal is to foster understanding and appreciation of the Cayuga Lake region and its ecosystems. With 100 acres of forests and fields to roam across, visitors have plenty of opportunities to have fun while learning about the natural world. The main lodge was built in 1939 and houses dozens of exhibits, including two, 650-gallon aquaria featuring the fishes of Cayuga Lake. A small number of animal ambassadors, all native species that cannot be returned to the wild due to injuries or illnesses, are kept at the center to help educate school groups and visitors. CNC hosts regular nature walks and science programs, a March maple tree celebration, and more. A highlight of the center is TreeTops, a six-story treehouse with stairs, ladders, cubby holes, and secret passageways to explore.

1420 Taughannock Blvd., 607-273-6260, cayuganaturecenter.org

77

CONNECT TO COMMUNITY ART

WITH ITHACA MURALS

Thanks to the Ithaca Murals nonprofit organization, empty walls across Ithaca are being transformed into gorgeous works of art. The project began with local artist Caleb Thomas, who ran a mural contest through the city's Public Art Commission in the mid-aughts. The success of the contest, and the resulting Underground Railroad–inspired mural by Jonathan Matas, instigated further investment in public art. With a focus on supporting diverse artists who create art that represents the local community, Thomas grew the initiative, founded Ithaca Murals, and has facilitated dozens more public art installations. Today, around 200 murals beautify the walls, fences, underpasses, bus stops, sidewalk electrical boxes, and schools throughout the city. Go down any street and you're bound to come across a mural, but a detailed map can be found and downloaded from the website and paper maps can be picked up at many establishments throughout Ithaca.

ithacamurals.com

78

LET THE WILDER BRAIN COLLECTION

BLOW YOUR MIND

In a nondescript hallway in one of Cornell University's many buildings, you'll find one of the weirdest things Ithaca has to offer: human brains. In 1889, Burt Green Wilder, a surgeon and professor of anatomy and neurology at Cornell, founded the Cornell Brain Society. For decades, he collected and researched brains. At one point during his work, the collection allegedly included 1,200 human and animal brains. Most of the collection was lost due to time and poor preservation, with the current collection retaining a few dozen. The Department of Psychology maintains most of the brains in storage, though eight brains are on display on the second floor of Uris Hall, alongside the biographies of their owners. You can see the preserved brains of several scientists and professors, suffragist Helen Hamilton Gardener, and Edward Rulloff, a 19th-century murderer. And don't miss Wilder's own brain, which, of course, he donated upon his death.

Uris Hall, Cornell University campus, 607-255-3834, psychology.cornell.edu

79

READ, CREATE, AND LEARN
AT THE TOMPKINS COUNTY PUBLIC LIBRARY

A treasured community resource, the Tompkins County Public Library is a welcoming space for everyone. The library was founded in 1864 by Ezra Cornell (founder of Cornell University) and was chartered and designated as the County Library in 1967. TCPL has thousands of print, electronic, and audio books and media, but it provides so much more. The central corridor serves as art space with rotating exhibits. The meeting rooms are year-round space for community events, film screenings, author visits, and presentations. TCPL offers programming for folks of all ages, like LEGO build night, teen youth groups, and book clubs, and it has a state-of-the-art makerspace with laser and 3D printers, sewing and Cricut machines, and craft tools. There is also a Library of Things, which loans out museum and park passes, chargers, calculators, and umbrellas. To make resources available for all, TCPL is a fine-free institution.

101 E Green St., 607-272-4557, tcpl.org

IMMERSE YOURSELF IN LITERATURE

AT THE SPRING WRITES LITERARY FESTIVAL

From Vladimir Nabokov to Toni Morrison to Diane Ackerman, Ithaca is known for the many literary greats who lived and wrote here. This is a community with an ongoing love of literature and each May, the Spring Writes Literary Festival brings out the literati from across the region. Coordinated by the Community Arts Partnership, the festival started out in 2009 as a small program with a handful of events. It now offers dozens of book readings, panel discussions, and storytelling performances by local writers, editors, artists, and organizations. An assortment of workshops are scheduled throughout May and into the summer. Events are held in locations around downtown including local bookstores and art galleries, the Tompkins County Public Library, and pubs and lounges. Most events are free and open to all, though some workshops require registration and a small fee.

Community Arts Partnership
607-273-5072, artspartner.org/content/view/spring-writes

JOURNEY INTO THE PAST
AT THE MUSEUM OF THE EARTH

When you see the North Atlantic right whale skeleton stretching 44 feet across the entryway at the Museum of the Earth, you know you've come to an extraordinary place. The Paleontological Research Institution opened the museum in 2003 for the community to learn about and enjoy earth science and natural history. As you descend to the museum's lower level, you'll pass artist Barbara Page's *Rock of Ages, Sands of Time* exhibit. This remarkable piece has 544 tiles, each representing one million years of geological time and depicting the organisms that existed throughout history. There are dozens of interactive permanent and rotating exhibits related to climate, dinosaurs, and geology. A must-see is the mastodon discovered in Hyde Park, New York, one of the world's most complete skeletons. Seeing the actual size of this massive creature that once roamed the earth gives a new perspective on our magnificent planet and its history.

1259 Trumansburg Rd., 607-273-6623, museumoftheearth.org

TIP

Calling all fossil lovers! Ithaca area streams and gorges are chock-full of fossils that you can easily find simply by turning over a rock. If you discover something that you need help identifying, bring it to the museum on the second Saturday of the month for Fossil ID Day. If you don't have your own, the museum's Fossil Lab allows you to dig through buckets of shale rocks and find fossils to examine, identify, and take home.

ENTER THE WHIMSICAL WORLD OF GOURDLANDIA

You've seen art made from paints, clay, and textiles, but have you experienced art made from a gourd? Gourdlandia is the creation of artist Graham Ottoson, a member of the American Gourd Society, who works from her unique studio on Ithaca's West Hill. She creates functional art like lamps and bowls, and imaginative art like masks and piñatas. Unlike other forms of art, this medium can be cultivated from seed to sculpture by the artist, and outside the studio, Ottoson tends a garden patch where she grows her own gourds. Stop by in spring to see the gourds sprouting or wander under the long trellis in summer with gourds hanging from the vines. The Gourdlandia shop offers plenty of art to purchase. Or register for a class where you can make your own night-light, globe lamp, box, or basket and see for yourself how fun and creative gourd art can be.

77 Rachel Carson Way, 607-277-0589, gourdlandia.com

PURSUE WISDOM
AT SAGE CHAPEL

Beauty, philosophy, inspiration—these are what you'll find when you visit Sage Chapel at Cornell University. The building opened in 1875 as a gift from Henry Williams Sage, one of Cornell's founders, and is a nondenominational Christian chapel, welcoming to all. The chapel holds a variety of religious services, but the intricate architectural details, the stained-glass windows, and the elaborate murals within convey the deeply held reverence for education as the highest ideal. Ella Condie Lamb's mosaic, unveiled in 1900, shows two trios of classically draped female figures representing the arts and sciences, with a central male figure representing philosophy. The Aeolian-Skinner organ was built for the chapel in 1940 and is regularly used for Glee Club and chorale concerts. Student recitals, weddings, and memorial services are also held here. Sage Chapel is the burial ground for founders of the university and has hosted renowned speakers including Martin Luther King Jr., Elie Wiesel, and Jane Goodall.

147 Ho Plaza, Cornell University campus, events.cornell.edu/sage_chapel

84

FOLLOW AN ART CRAWL
ON FIRST FRIDAY GALLERY NIGHTS

Why go to one art gallery when you can go to a dozen? On the first Friday of each month, meander among the galleries and shops that open their doors for special evening art shows and opening receptions. The shows feature painters, sculptors, photographers, and printmakers from across the region and country. Exhibits change from month to month so you'll likely see new artists every first Friday. Other shops and galleries not in the downtown vicinity also get in on the fun, though you'll have to drive there. Check out the Downtown Ithaca Alliance's downloadable map, which serves as a guide to the artists and venues. The galleries are open throughout the month, so if you can't make it to First Friday, stop by and see the art on your own schedule.

Downtown Ithaca Alliance
607-277-8679, ithacagallerynight.com

SOME DOWNTOWN GALLERIES TO VISIT

State of the Art Gallery
120 W State St., 607-277-1626
soagithaca.org

MIX Art Gallery
156 E State St., on the Commons, 607-319-4364
mixartgallery.com

Community School of Music and Arts Gallery
330 E State St., 607-272-1474
csma-ithaca.org/gallery

Petrune Gallery
126 E State St., 2nd Floor, on the Commons, 607-279-2161
petrunegallery.com

Community Arts Partnership ArtSpace
110 N Tioga St., on the Commons, 607-273-5072
artspartner.org/content/view/artspace.html

REACH THE STARS
ALONG THE SAGAN PLANET WALK

Comprehending the size of our solar system can be mind-boggling, but the Sagan Planet Walk brings those incomprehensible numbers to a human scale. This walkable, one-to-five-billion scale model extends 1.2 kilometers (0.75 miles) through downtown Ithaca. Our sun, a yellow dwarf star, is represented by a stone obelisk at the center of the Commons. The inner planet stations are a few steps away, while you'll have to head around the block and keep going to find the outer planets, ending at dwarf planet Pluto at the Sciencenter. Read the informational graphics and listen to the audio tour, narrated by Bill Nye, the Science Guy. The Planet Walk was created, in part, to honor Carl Sagan, renowned astronomer, astrophysicist, and Pulitzer Prize winning author. Sagan lived in Ithaca and taught at Cornell University from the 1970s until his death in 1996. He is buried in Ithaca's Lakeview Cemetery.

Start at the Ithaca Commons, end at 1st Street at the Sciencenter
607-272-0600, saganplanetwalk.com

TIP

Alpha Centauri, the star nearest our sun, is about 40 trillion kilometers away. In 2012, a station was added to the Sagan Planet Walk scale model to represent Alpha Centauri. If you want to visit this stop, you'll need to travel to the 'Imiloa Astronomy Center in Hilo, Hawai'i, where the information station further explores the vast distances of space.

Dewitt Mall

SHOPPING AND FASHION

86

SAVOR THE SEASON
AT ITHACA FARMERS MARKET

A perfect summer Saturday morning means ambling the bustling stalls of the Ithaca Farmers Market, filling your grocery bags with the best local goods, and filling your belly with the yummiest hot foods. Since 1973, growers, artists, and vendors have come from a 30-mile radius to sell everything from in-season fruits and vegetables to silk-screened clothing to bakery items to fresh-cut and potted flowers to local wines and ciders and much more. The market is located on the banks of the Cayuga Lake inlet at Steamboat Landing. The open-air pavilion, built in 1988, protects from the spring rainy days and catches the cool breezes off the lake on the steamy summer days. Hot-food vendors fill many of the stalls, but get there early to avoid the long lines at lunchtime. There's outdoor seating aplenty, and local musicians provide a festive environment for shopping and snacking.

545 3rd St., 607-273-7109, ithacamarket.com

TIP

At Steamboat Landing, the Saturday market runs April through December and the Sunday market runs May through November. There are smaller summer markets on Tuesdays downtown and Wednesdays on East Hill. The winter market operates out of Triphammer Marketplace from January through March. Always check the website for specific times, dates, and locations.

87

SAMPLE EXCELLENCE
AT ITHACA COFFEE COMPANY

Are you looking for a cup of rich, locally roasted coffee? Or maybe you want to try an exclusive craft beer? How about some imported candies, artisan cheeses, or gourmet meats? You'll find all this and more under one roof at the Ithaca Coffee Company. The company started roasting coffee beans in Ithaca in 1984 as Gourmet's Delight but changed ownership in 2004. Keeping the former operation's dedication to specialty, premium coffee, the Ithaca Coffee Company was born and expanded their market into craft beers and premium retail foodstuffs. The full-service espresso bar has a cozy seating area to catch up with a friend, while the tavern has a warm, inviting atmosphere and offers weekly beer tastings. The retail shelves are stocked with hundreds of quality sweets, snacks, oils, and preserves. ICC also goes all in for the holidays with gift baskets and everything you need to set a delicious holiday table.

2255 Triphammer Rd., in Triphammer Marketplace, 607-257-2626
ithacacoffee.com

TAKE A TRIP DOWN MEMORY LANE
AT THE HISTORIC DEWITT MALL

Wander through the Dewitt Mall and you may feel like you've been transported to a bygone era, with all the modern-day amenities. Prolific architect William Henry Miller built the four-story building in 1914 in the Collegiate Gothic style popular at the time. The imposing stone building was the Ithaca High School until the 1960s, then the Dewitt Junior High School until the 1970s when it was repurposed. These days, contemporary Ithaca meets old-school history in a city planner's multiuse dream. On the first floor, local merchants sell goods like clothing, antiques, guitars, and gifts, while the mouthwatering scents from several eateries fill the air. Upper levels are rented as offices and apartments. As you're eating, strolling, and shopping in the mall, take note of the original architectural features adorning the building, including carvings above the entrance doors, large, multipaned windows, and stone staircases worn down by thousands of feet.

215 N Cayuga St., 607-273-6464, thedewittmall.com

SOME OF THE STOPS IN DEWITT MALL FOR SHOPPING AND EATING

Café Dewitt
607-273-3473, cafedewitt.com

Pastimes Antiques
607-277-3457, pastimes.com

Ithaca Guitar Works
607-272-2602, guitarworks.com

Ithacamade
607-272-1396, facebook.com/ithacamade

89

AMUSE YOURSELF
AT ALPHABET SOUP

No matter your age, shopping for toys at Alphabet Soup will add cheer to your day. An Ithaca staple since 1984, Alphabet Soup prides itself on its array of premium-quality, specialty, and good old-fashioned toys. Wandering the colorful aisles (or the online store), you'll find big-name toys and books from LEGO, Ravensburger, and Usborne, but you're equally likely to find goods that are locally made, eco-friendly, and made for kids of varying abilities. The front counter is covered with bits and bobs and lots of little things for little hands. And if you want to just play it simple, there are kites, beach balls, and markers too. Alphabet Soup values community partnerships and donates toys to local organizations, nonprofits, and fundraisers like Cops, Kids & Toys. Their commitment shows, with the Downtown Ithaca Alliance honoring the shop's owner, Greta Perl, with the 2020 Retailer of the Year Award.

171 E State St., on the Commons, 607-272-6885, alphabetsoupithaca.com

TWO OTHER FUN TOY SHOPS

The Cat's Pajamas
99 E Seneca St., in Dewitt Mall 607-272-5582, catspajamasithaca.com

The Brain Shoppe
210 E State St., on the Commons 607-277-2757, thebrainshoppe.com

90

FIND THE PERFECT FIT
AT FONTANA'S

For more than 100 years, Fontana's shoe store has been outfitting the feet of Ithacans with fashionable shoes. Italian immigrant Cesare Fontana opened the shop in 1907, starting out as a cobbler, repairing shoes. By the 1940s, Fontana was selling shoes as well. The business passed through generations of the Fontana family until 2002, when Shawn Manning, who had previously worked with the family, took over management of the store. Fontana's has shoes for every style and popular brands like Birkenstock, Keen, Merrell, Teva, Ecco, Saucony, and more. They also specialize in shoes for wide and hard-to-fit feet. Staying true to their founder's origins, Fontana's continues to offer repair services like resoling, reheeling, cleaning, and polishing. Fontana's has a devoted following because of the staff's experience and excellent service. Their slogan says it all: "On Eddy Street in Collegetown—since before you were born."

401 Eddy St., 607-272-7255, fontanas-shoes.com

RUMMAGE FOR TREASURE
AT THE FINGER LAKES REUSE CENTER

Each year, thousands of perfectly good household items are thrown in the trash that could instead be repurposed or reused. With a commitment to community, affordability, and waste reduction, Finger Lakes ReUse offers a new vision for a community-centered economy. Businesses and residents donate used goods, and the ReUse team organizes it all into two giant warehouse stores. The buildings are always abuzz with shoppers searching for treasures. The Elmira Road store has everything from kitchen goods to sporting gear to toys to craft supplies to electronics to building supplies. The Triphammer Marketplace location, the ReUse Megacenter, carries an array of clothing and textile items, jewelry, home decor, and furniture. Check out the Fixers Collective, which offers opportunities to bring in broken items, like a toy car, old lamp, or radio, and get help fixing it. Become a Super ReUser and get 10 percent off the already low prices on everything in the store.

214 Elmira Rd.
2255 N Triphammer Rd., in Triphammer Marketplace
607-257-9699, ithacareuse.org

TIP

Check out Historic Ithaca's architectural salvage store, Significant Elements. It's a gold mine for antiques, vintage decor, period furniture, and unique building materials.

212 Center St., 607-277-3450, significantelements.org

GAIN ENLIGHTENMENT
AT BUFFALO STREET BOOKS

Ithaca has been dubbed the "most enlightened" city by various sources and polls. No doubt a contributing factor is the dedication to learning and education and the love of independent bookstores. A longtime, indispensable shop is Buffalo Street Books, opened as the Bookery II in 1991. When the owners announced the store's closure in the early 2010s, the community pulled together hundreds of thousands of dollars to buy it out and turn it into a consumer-owned cooperative. Its shelves are filled with literary classics as well as new releases, and the downtown space is a hub of bookish activity. On any given week you can attend a variety of readings, workshops, book clubs, and story times. Anyone can shop at the store, but if you really want to be a part of the action, become a member-owner and boast to your friends that you own a bookstore!

215 N Cayuga St., in Dewitt Mall, 607-273-8246, buffalostreetbooks.com

OTHER ENLIGHTENING BOOKSTORES

Odyssey Bookstore
115 W Green St., 607-269-5800
odysseybookstore.com

One Green Horse Used Books
9 E Main St., Trumansburg
607-387-7200

Autumn Leaves Used Bookstore
115 E State St., on the Commons, 607-273-8239
blog.pmpress.org/autumn-leaves-bookstore

93

HEAD OFF THE BEATEN PATH
TO BROOKTON'S MARKET

Unwind from your busy workaday life by visiting Brookton's Market, a classic country store just a few miles outside of Ithaca at the heart of the quaint hamlet of Brooktondale. While it has been in its current iteration since 2007, the building itself, complete with creaky wooden floors and high ceilings, has operated as a store since the 1880s. The popular neighborhood venue always has brewed coffee ready to go, and locals gather for the live music, trivia, and family events every week. If you're hungry, choose from sandwiches, baked goods, or deli fare and settle into a big wooden booth. The grocery is stocked with farm-fresh produce and dairy, daily necessities, and handmade wares from local artists and crafters. At the end of a long day, relax on the outdoor patio with your friends while you sip a glass of local wine or one of the 24 craft beers on tap.

491 Brooktondale Rd., Brooktondale, 607-539-7900, brooktonsmarket.com

94

SATIATE YOUR PASSION FOR ART
AT HANDWORK ARTISAN COOPERATIVE

Entering Handwork, where vibrantly colored pottery, dangly floral earrings, and perfectly inlaid wooden cutting boards will instantly catch your eye, you'll realize that Ithaca is overflowing with creativity. In 1976, a dozen craftspeople joined forces to start Handwork, Ithaca's Artist Cooperative. The goal, like many other cooperatives that began in the 1970s, was to pool resources and set up a retail storefront to jointly sell their work. Now, more than 30 artists from the Finger Lakes region are members who run the operation, staff the sales desk, and talk with customers. The art includes fabric work, photography, leatherwork, silk-screen design, basketry, glasswork, and more. If you stop by when the store is closed, the window shopping will tide you over because Handwork uses its prominent storefront windows to highlight community events, promote visiting artists, and present a rotating display of work from Black, Indigenous, and People of Color artisans.

102 W State St., 607-273-9400, handwork.coop

BECOME A BIBLIOPHILE
AT THE FRIENDS OF THE LIBRARY BOOK SALE

Over three long weekends in May and another three in October, the Friends of the Tompkins County Public Library holds one of the biggest used book sales in the country. Inside the giant blue warehouse, an army of volunteers organizes the books into every genre you can think of, and some you didn't know existed. There's a huge children's section, along with sections of games, records, and DVDs. Donations come from libraries, schools, and households, and an average of 200,000 items pass through the warehouse during each sale. The first weekend, items are priced at $4.50, with prices dropping each subsequent weekend. Proceeds go to the Tompkins County Public Library, the Finger Lakes Library System, and other nonprofit organizations promoting reading and literacy. On the final Monday of the sale, every item costs a dime. The final Tuesday of the sale is bag day; fill a grocery bag full of books for only a dollar.

509 Esty St., 607-272-2223, booksale.org

TIP

Every year, a handmade quilt, often with a bookish theme, is displayed at the entrance to the building. Folks can buy raffle tickets, and at the end of the sale, one lucky winner will take the quilt home. The proceeds also go to support the Friends' activities and grants.

96

SHOP GREEN
AT GREENSTAR FOOD CO-OP

GreenStar Food Co-op, founded in 1971 as the Ithaca Real Food Co-op, essentially began as a group of friends who ordered wholesale bulk foods and drove them in from Syracuse. The cooperative expanded and by the 1980s had a retail storefront called the Grain Store, which was eventually renamed GreenStar. The large bulk department is still the heart of GreenStar, but the co-op also has a grocery featuring local and national brands, a local produce department, a wellness department of cruelty-free and natural products and supplements, and a prepared foods department with everything from sushi to hot mac and cheese to made-to-order sandwiches. Don't miss the bakery, with its assortment of vegan goods, including a swoon-worthy vegan chocolate cake. The co-op is member owned with an elected board, but you don't have to be a member to shop there. GreenStar is all about community and everyone is welcome.

770 Cascadilla St., 607-273-9392
307 College Ave., 607-882-2667
215 N Cayuga St., in Dewitt Mall, 607-273-8213
greenstar.coop

DISCOVER MICRO-RETAIL
AT PRESS BAY ALLEY

Press Bay Alley gets its name from the space itself. The long, narrow building and alleyway were once owned by the Ithaca Journal, and the storage bays were used to store newspapers. With creative readaptation in mind, developer John Guttridge renovated the space, replacing the garage doors of each bay with glass and transforming the space to allow for new and vibrant uses. With outdoor tables and chairs, the courtyard is cozy and perfect for socializing with friends. In 2018, the Press Bay footprint expanded to Press Bay Court, a half block east, allowing for another group of micro-retailers to set up shop. Combined, the two areas offer a unique downtown shopping experience. In addition to the year-round stores, Press Bay serves as a pickup location for local CSAs (community-supported agriculture) and hosts events and pop-up shopping like the Holiday Local Food Market, artisan markets, and other community events.

116 W Green St. and 110 W Green St., pressbayalley.com

A FEW OF THE SHOPS TO VISIT AT PRESS BAY

Press Cafe
presscafeithaca.com

Rashida Sawyer Bakery
607-233-4061, rashidasawyer.com

Sew Green
607-319-4106, sewgreenithaca.com

Mama Said Hand Pies
607-280-5941, mamasaidhandpies.com

PLAY ALL DAY
AT MAMA GOOSE AND JILLIAN'S DRAWERS

Two Ithaca essentials, Mama Goose and Jillian's Drawers, share one large, bright space that is a maze of children's books, clothes, toys, and shoes. Mama Goose was founded in 2003, thanks to two moms with a dream to open a children's resale store. Jillian's Drawers began with a mom who worked from home helping parents with cloth diapers and eventually opened a storefront in 2008. With overlapping goals and similar patrons, the supermom professionals of these stores joined forces when Jillian's owner purchased Mama Goose in 2020 and moved them to a common location. Jillian's focuses on newborn, baby, and maternity items, while Mama Goose takes on toddlers and older-kid gear. The beauty is that you'll find great deals on gently used items while also discovering new clothes and toys all in one place. The stores also offer a community room and play space with weekly classes and events for moms, kids, and families.

Mama Goose
609 W Clinton St., 607-216-7851, mamagooseithaca.com

Jillian's Drawers
609 W Clinton St., 607-272-1237, jilliansdrawers.com

TIP

If you'd rather borrow toys to play with, visit the Finger Lakes Toy Library. Toys for all ages line the shelves and can be checked out for several weeks at a time. This uncommon lending organization offers the joy of play to everyone who enters its doors.

Shops at Ithaca Mall
40 Catherwood Rd., Ste. D07, 607-319-0488
fingerlakestoylibrary.org

99

STROLL AND SHOP
THE ITHACA COMMONS

Central to the identity of Ithaca is the Commons, a pedestrian mall lined by historic brick buildings filled with shops, restaurants, and entertainment. The Commons coincides with State Street, a.k.a. Martin Luther King Jr. Street, the city's original main drag for horse-drawn carriages and sleighs in the 19th century and clattering trolleys in the early 1900s. Cars zipped through until the 1960s when city planners and politicians decided to try something drastically different. They closed the road to traffic, then renovated the street by adding pavilions, a fountain, and trees. People flocked to the new pedestrian mall, which is now the site of many festivals, concerts, rallies, and events. A mid-2010s makeover added a new playground and fountain, redesigned the Bernie Milton Pavilion stage, and installed high-efficiency LED lighting and native plant beds. The stores, eateries, and galleries have changed over the years, but no matter the decade, the Commons will always carry the distinct, charming spirit of Ithaca.

downtownithaca.com/visit-downtown/the-commons

SHOPS NOT TO MISS

Sunny Days of Ithaca
171 E State St., on the Commons, 607-319-5260
sunnydaysny.com

The Outdoor Store
206 E State St., on the Commons, 607-273-3891

Mockingbird Paperie
144 E State St., on the Commons, 607-319-0556
mockingbirdpaperie.com

15 Steps
171 E State St., on the Commons, 607-272-4902
fifteensteps.com

Home Green Home
126 E. State St., on the Commons, 607-319-4159
homegreenhome.com

Angry Mom Records
115 E State St., on the Commons, 607-319-4953
angry-mom-records.com

100

STOP AND SMELL THE ROSES
AT BOOL'S FLOWER SHOP

It is a rare thing that lasts 130 years, but Bool's Flower Shop is one of those things. Opened in 1894, Bool's has long been creating floral beauty for the community and is one of Ithaca's oldest shops of any kind. They offer small and large traditional floral arrangements for weddings, birthdays, funerals, and proms, but they also create contemporary designs for any other event you might imagine. Bool's does more than sell flowers; they are a distinctive participant in the community. They have hosted a theater production of *Little Shop of Horrors* in their shop, shared bouquets for Petal It Forward (a flower giveaway to unsuspecting passersby to promote kindness), and participated in the Downtown First Friday Gallery Night. Bool's also has gift baskets, chocolates, other plants and succulents, and candles. They deliver daily throughout the area.

209 N Aurora St., 607-272-8410, boolsflowershop.com

ACTIVITIES
BY SEASON

SPRING

SUMMER

FALL

WINTER

SUGGESTED ITINERARIES

ICONIC ITHACA

FOR ANIMAL LOVERS

FREE AND LOW-COST ACTIVITIES

FUN FOR KIDS

OUT OF THE ORDINARY ENJOYMENT

DATE NIGHT

ON THE WATERFRONT

EXPLORE THE NATURAL WORLD

FOR SPORTS FANS

BEYOND THE BOUNDS OF THE CITY

INDEX